Literature—News That Stays News

Literature—News That Stays News

Fresh Approaches to the Classics

Classroom Practices in Teaching English 1984

Candy Carter, Chair,

and the Committee on Classroom Practices

National Council of Teachers of English
1111 Kenyon Road, Urbana, Illinois 61801

NCTE Editorial Board: Julie M. Jensen, Delores Lipscomb, John S. Mayher, Elisabeth McPherson, John C. Maxwell, *ex officio,* Paul O'Dea, *ex officio*

Staff Editor: Lee Erwin

Book Design: Tom Kovacs for TGK Design

NCTE Stock Number 30127

Library of Congress Cataloging in Publication Data

Main entry under title:

Literature—news that stays news.

   (Classroom practices in teaching English; 1984)
   Bibliography: p.
   1. Literature—Study and teaching.   I. Carter,
Candy, 1947–   .   II. National Council of Teachers
of English. Committee on Classroom Practices.
III. Series.
PN59.L54   1985   807   84–27369
ISBN 0–8141–3012–7

Contents

5 Units for Specific Titles: College

Preface

Our 1982–83 Classroom Practices Committee meetings were held at a time when writing was a primary concern of English teachers throughout the country. "Jill and Johnny can't read" had been replaced by "Jill and Johnny can't write, either," in the frightening headlines in newspapers and magazines. The proliferation of writing projects across the country had brought about a revolution in teachers' approaches to the writing process and a new awareness of how our students learn to respond on paper. However, having devoted so much time and energy to the teaching of writing and the study of the teaching of writing, many teachers across the nation, it seemed, were neglecting the teaching of literature. Class sets of old favorites were moldering on shelves. Was it possible, however, that as a result of our reawakened interest in writing, new approaches had been found to improve the teaching of literature as well? This was the hope of our committee when we met at the national convention in 1982 and again at the spring convention in 1983.

After our spring meeting, the call for manuscripts was issued in *Language Arts, English Journal, Council-Grams, College English,* and *English Education,* as well as in the journals of many NCTE-affiliated organizations. By December 1, we had received dozens of manuscripts from teachers throughout the country. The manuscripts, with authors' names removed, were evaluated by committee members Jean Procope-Martin, James Lalley, Patricia Phelan, and Yetive Bradley—a committee representing several geographic areas and grade levels.

Twenty-nine manuscripts representing these varying viewpoints were finally selected and submitted to the NCTE Editorial Board for approval to publish. All of them represent fresh approaches to old favorites. The committee hopes this volume will help provide new methods to bring those old friends, the classics, into the lives of students.

Introduction

We often become embroiled in a definition of the term *classic*. Can we simply say that good literature is "news that *stays* news" (Ezra Pound)? Unlike a flashy headline on a day-old paper, the classics repay attention time and again.

Like every other teacher, I want my students to enjoy reading. However, like others of my teaching generation in the seventies and early eighties, I sometimes denied students the satisfaction of wrestling with a difficult but important classic in my efforts to find "relevant" or "motivational" material. I realized there was a problem when not one student in my gifted class had read *Little Women, Treasure Island,* or any of a host of other children's classics. Most of these students had parents who fostered reading at home; they were students who could read nearly anything put into their hands. Yet they were culturally deprived in the true sense of the phrase, and I had to take part of the blame.

We must take a look at what place teaching the classics takes in our "megatrend" society. Can we justify Shakespeare and Homer when the knowledge a student must consume simply to survive increases geometrically every year? Robert Polhemus, Stanford English department chair, in "Welcome to the English Department" (*Stanford English Department Newsletter* 3, no. 1 [Autumn 1981]), defines the "use" of English most aptly:

> Utilitarian emphasis . . . would really be only trendy rationalization for taking English. . . . Literature is meant to move your heart, change or clarify your mind, and bring you closer to the whole sprawling community of particular history, language and imagination—the human conditions. . . . [Through literature] you'll find your deepest soul touched and defined, you'll sense an explosion of meaning in yourself, and you'll better know your own humanity and what it might signify. There could be no better educational purpose or experience.

It simply would not work to bring out lesson plans from 1960 and inflict them on students in the 1980s and 1990s. We have learned too much and come too far for that. The contributions contained in this volume are a clear demonstration that the teaching of literature is alive and well, that some of us have continued to teach the classics and have applied our new knowledge of the most effective language arts methods to reawaken an interest in those works that form a part of our human heritage.

Classic books, like classic cars, classic clothes, and classical music, are always appealing. We find ourselves returning to these books like old friends. We are comfortable with them. We learn something new from them every time. And that is "news that stays news."

Candy Carter
Sierra Mountain Intermediate
    School
Truckee, California

1 Linking the Classics: Approaches to Multiple Titles

Golding as a Key to Conrad

Jane A. Beem
Warren Township High School, Gurnee, Illinois

When I considered using one of Joseph Conrad's short novels in a high-school honors course, I recalled my own perplexing first exposure to Conrad. Perhaps some of my confusion arose from the obscure kinds of questions I was required to answer. Perhaps some of my problems evolved because I was left to wing it on my own for the most part, not having had the benefit of class discussion. Yet I felt that adding Conrad to the repertoire of these bright high-schoolers had merit; however, I wanted, as much as possible, to spare them the uncertainties I had experienced. I wanted them to enjoy reading Conrad's work.

We were already reading William Golding's *Lord of the Flies,* a novel students enjoy reading because of its exotic adventure and because it touches base, especially near the beginning, with their own childhood games and play. (And now that Golding has become a Nobel Prize-winner for literature, his novel should generate new interest.) *Lord of the Flies,* furthermore, raises questions about human nature and societal problems that trigger lively discussion. As I thought about Golding's novel while planning the next semester's readings, the statement, "Ralph wept for the end of innocence, the darkness of man's heart"[1] suggested to me a connection with Conrad's *Heart of Darkness,* so I decided to teach *Lord of the Flies* and *Heart of Darkness* together, since thematically the two novels have a great deal in common. After reading *Lord of the Flies,* and discussing a little background information on Conrad so that students would recognize the autobiographical influence in the story, we tackled *Heart of Darkness.* Students handled the reading surprisingly well.

We begin this unit by spending one class period doing an impromptu writing on the topic, "What I would do if I were leader of a group stranded on an island." This activity requires students to think seriously about leadership and responsibility. The following day I read the impromptus aloud to the class. (When I read student writing aloud to the class, I never reveal the name of the writer, but I usually tell them that if

3

they'd like to take a bow after I read theirs, they are welcome to do so. This practice seems to meet the needs of both the shy and the gregarious in the class.) Students enjoy hearing the variety of ideas presented in these impromptus, and I am pleased that some express the same priorities Ralph had in *Lord of the Flies,* and some those Jack had, while a few are still "littluns" who only see how much fun it could be being stranded on a tropical island. At this point, however, I don't let them in on my delight. I simply encourage them to remember these ideas and to look at the writings again later to see who comes closest to Golding's insights into the dilemma of being stranded, which ultimately lead the reader to his rather grim view of human nature.

The reading of *Lord of the Flies* goes rather quickly and we discuss the novel after everyone in the class is finished. In discussing the whole novel, I field questions from students first because honors students are generally full of questions when they finish this novel. To encourage this I have each student write one question on a piece of paper and bring it to class the following day. Also, I frequently throw out comments critics have made about the novel and ask students to explain why they agree or disagree with each statement. Discussion of the novel is stimulating, as a rule, since students themselves raise ethical questions about human nature. The Ralphs in the class criticize the foolishness of the hunters, while the Jacks in the class tend to recognize Ralph's weaknesses as a leader and the weakness of people in general.

The reading of *Heart of Darkness* progresses a little more slowly because the language and allusions are more complex and the setting is strange to most students, but the novel is short and can be read in a week and a half comfortably. With *Heart of Darkness* it is more important to have daily discussion in order for students to absorb the story and to clarify details than it is with *Lord of the Flies.* For instance, students may need a bit of explanation about the Roman conquest of Britain to understand the significance of the beginning of Marlow's story. Also, a map might help them visualize his journey. Occasionally, clarification can come through reference to similarities in *Lord of the Flies.* Upon completion of the reading of *Heart of Darkness,* the class can compare the two novels in detail. Students by this time should readily recognize the common concern of the two authors.

Ralph's reference to "the darkness of man's heart," particularly, leads to extensive discussion of both novels. Not only does it stimulate discussion of the flaws in human nature exemplified by Jack, Roger, and Kurtz—and even by the morally responsible such as Ralph at fleeting moments—but it leads to discussion of imagery as well, especially in *Heart of Darkness.* Conrad explores darkness from many angles. As Marlow, the storyteller, rambles on to his small group of companions on board the yacht *Nellie,* he reflects on those who conquered what came to be known as England, comparing them with more recent conquerors. He points out that conquerors in whatever age have had to "tackle a darkness."[2] Yet he suggests that the cruelty with which they conquer the savage, mysterious, incomprehensible darkness is in itself a kind of darkness—one of blindness, perhaps of ignorance, certainly of insensitivity and fear of the unknown. In both novels the darkness of the jungle generates such fear. For the young boys the beast resides there; for Marlow unfamiliar eyes cloaked in foliage watch as he travels upstream. He knows not whether they are friendly or hostile; the answer can be found only by penetrating the darkness. In both stories the journey into a more primitive way of life is a journey into darkness. Ignorance, mystery, evil, death—all are symbolized by darkness and all play a role in both novels.

An outgrowth of the idea of the darkness within humans, the theme of "man's inhumanity to man," is developed in both novels. Though both stories show the residual effects of civilization, these become mere remnants as the characters remove themselves further and further from society. For example, early in *Lord of the Flies* Roger throws stones in a circle around Percival, one of the younger boys, but at that point the restraints of civilization prevent him from hitting the child with a stone. Later in the novel, however, Roger viciously rolls a boulder onto Piggy, murdering the most rational person on the island. In another episode, the boys wildly attack and kill Simon, whose deep insight and intuition could have relieved their ignorance and fear of the beast. Cruelty, ignorance, and darkness prevail. Similarly, in *Heart of Darkness* Marlow sees a progression from order, exemplified by the elegant appearance of the chief accountant at the first station, to the stealthiness of the "papier-mâché Mephistopheles" (p. 39) who manages the central station, to the ruthless power of Kurtz at the inner station. The deeper Marlow penetrates the heart of darkness, the fewer are the residual effects of civilization. In the end Kurtz can only recall his experience with the words, "the horror" (p. 111). The darkness of evil prevails. The shrunken heads on the fenceposts around his house evidence that.

Golding said, "The shape of a society must depend on the ethical nature of the individual and not on any political system however apparently logical or respectable" (p. 189). Golding develops this theme in *Lord of the Flies* when Ralph's democratic system cannot prevail against the power of Jack's personality, whereby the unethical nature of one individual leads the boys into savagery. Some willingly follow; some are very likely coerced into following. Golding's statement is also true of *Heart of Darkness.* Kurtz has been out of touch with society for some time (the reason for Marlow's mission). While Conrad never makes clear what "the horror" is, it is apparent that Kurtz's personality, like Jack's, controls the "island" in the jungle known as the inner station and its surrounding area. He has somehow shaped that society to produce large quantities of ivory for him. Has he done so ethically? The shrunken heads on the fenceposts call his behavior into question, as does his repetition of "the horror." And though the remaining natives seemed loyal to Kurtz, it remains a fact that he is exploiting these people. Despite their exploitative nature, Jack and Kurtz win the following of their respective groups.

Using *Lord of the Flies* as a doorway into *Heart of Darkness* can generate interest in the latter. If students are challenged to look for similarities, the reading of *Heart of Darkness* becomes something of a game. There is adventure in discovery, so I give students a chance to discover as many similarities as they can before I make suggestions. The discussion of *Lord of the Flies* can be largely student-dominated, as suggested above, whereas the teacher needs to serve as a resource person during discussion of *Heart of Darkness*. The study of these two novels together has been rewarding for me as a teacher, and I believe that *Lord of the Flies* has helped students to see *Heart of Darkness* more clearly.

Notes

1. William Golding, *Lord of the Flies* (New York: Capricorn, 1959), 186-87. Subsequent page references are to this edition.

2. Joseph Conrad, *Heart of Darkness* (New York: Pocket Books, 1972), 7. Subsequent page references are to this edition.

Grendel: Monster or Adolescent?

Joseph Bonfiglio
Green Mountain Union High School, Chester, Vermont

Each fall my advanced-placement British literature class reads and studies *Beowulf* and John Gardner's *Grendel* (New York: Knopf, 1971) during the first three weeks of the term. Our study of *Beowulf* is traditional, focusing on plot, theme, and historical background, section by section, for five class periods. I have prepared the students for this with an introductory lecture and presentation of other short pieces from the Anglo-Saxon period, and we listen to recordings of these pieces in their original dialect.

At the end of our treatment of *Beowulf,* rather than going on to discuss *Grendel,* I ask my students to write a one- or two-page essay on the topic "Is Grendel a Monster?" making a specific choice, rather than an argument for both sides of the question. The next time the class meets, the students share their essays in small groups. They usually argue about which answer is the "correct" one. Then, I ask each group to pick the best essay, and the student selected reads it to the class. Criticizing these papers on the strength of their arguments, I ask my students to do the same.

The class will usually split down the middle on the question (except for one or two students who choose both alternatives) and will forcefully ask me for the "correct" response. When I tell them there isn't one, I usually have to deal with a short interlude of anarchy. However, I eventually focus the class discussion on several major items. We discuss how to attack a question like this one. Most students agree that they must define *monster* and that they are not necessarily held captive by the dictionary. Next, we discuss using the text to support a thesis. Usually, students who have said Grendel is a monster have gotten most of their information from *Beowulf.*

This leads us into a discussion of point of view as a literary device. Gardner's book is written in the first person and is a good illustration of this structural technique. Point of view takes us into a discussion of prejudice, a theme that appears in both works, although more so in

Grendel. Students usually recognize how point of view can bias a person. The proof of this is that Gardner is obviously sympathetic toward Grendel; most of the students who feel that Grendel is not a monster use Gardner's book as their primary resource. I then suggest that the students read Michael Crichton's *Eaters of the Dead,* the same narrative from a third point of view.

After we have examined all of these possibilities in detail, I tell the students that I am going to present to them a major thesis that I have been working on for years and that I am readying for publication. Although most of this isn't true, it's fun to say so anyway. I write a thesis statement on the board: "In the book *Grendel,* John Gardner portrays the title character as an exaggerated view of adolescence."

I am immediately greeted with laughter. Even though I am not totally serious, I state that I am and reiterate this after every major point. There is laughter after every point, and its intensity grows, but the laughter is directly related to interest.

I list the major points in succession, emphasizing each with a brief vignette about adolescence in general or my adolescence in particular. I cite Grendel's fascination with his own appearance. We discuss how peer groups work and how cliques evolve (Grendel can't break into the clique). Grendel's unrealistic sexual feelings and fantasies concerning Wealhtheow are compared to school dance courtship rituals. Students often cite Grendel's inability to communicate with most of the "adult" Danes. Grendel's lair takes on both the appearance and the womb-like quality of the average teenager's room. The ambivalent relationship between adolescent and parent (in this case, Grendel's mother) is another point of discussion. Some students identify the dragon as the representative of the overwhelming influence of peers on adolescents. Other points touched on are fear, egocentrism, bullying, ego gratification, and even voyeurism.

To tie together all of our brainstorming, I ask students to define alienation and apply the definition to Grendel. I then ask them to compare in writing the characters in *Grendel* and the characters in *Lord of the Flies,* which most of them have read one or two years earlier.

The object of this unit is to get students to think, to interpret, to criticize, and to debate the contents of the books. I also get them to write two significant expository essays which are, ideally, developed logically using the available text. They work together and examine their own environments and value systems. Finally, I try to get them to enjoy these books. I'm pretty sure they do. This week, five seniors who aren't in my class asked me if they could read *Grendel* because they had heard it is good!

The Misfit in Literature: A Course That Links Some Interesting Classics

Diane Wilson
St. John's School, Houston, Texas

One Flew Over the Cuckoo's Nest, Light in August, Madame Bovary, and *Hamlet.* These were the works that I felt had been consistently worthwhile in the various one-semester elective high-school courses I had taught under such different titles as "Shakespeare," "Contemporary Fiction," and "The Novel." When asked, "Which book that we read had the most impact on you and/or changed your thinking on some issue(s)?" students cited these four over and over, so I decided to organize a thematically united course called "The Misfit in Literature." These four texts form an interesting and stimulating unit, and this course is an effective way to expose students of quite different abilities to these important, rich classics.

I teach the works in the fall semester in inverse chronological order (as they are listed above). The advantage to this approach is that students are so captivated by the first one, Ken Kesey's *Cuckoo's Nest,* that the teacher can use the goodwill and enthusiasm established to get them into William Faulkner's *Light in August,* which, though more difficult, has some similarities in its unconventional narrative method and point of view. Dealing with the limitations and advantages of Chief Bromden as the narrator of *Cuckoo's Nest* opens up the concept of the shifting and biased point of view that is more complicated in *Light in August.* The various reasons for the patients' not being able to fit into society get students thinking about the power of the environment to break down self-love; they are therefore more capable of understanding Joe Christmas's agony at his ambiguous racial background as well as his devastating exposure to sex and religion. Further, the brutality, both emotional and physical, of the activities on Nurse Ratched's ward prepares students for the horrifying inhumanity in Faulkner.

Madame Bovary and *Hamlet* are almost a relief to me and to my students after the twentieth-century books. Why that is the case is an interesting area to explore. Besides the obvious questions of why Emma and Hamlet do not fit into their worlds and what the writers are saying through their alienation, Gustave Flaubert's novel and William Shakespeare's tragedy have in common remarkable imagery, much of which is related to disease and decay. (By the way, the idea of the disgusting, ugly machine that obsesses the narrator in *Cuckoo's Nest* is suggested at several points in *Light in August,* and there are Christ figures in both *Cuckoo's Nest* and *Light in August.*) If imagery is not for every student group, then the contrast of the sensitive, lucid, self-questioning misfit, Hamlet, with Emma, who doesn't know herself and who lacks sensitivity and passion, and doesn't even know that, is accessible to most.

Most advantageous in this method of organizing an English course is the feature of students' being intrigued by the protagonists and their problems. They don't *like* them all—thank heavens! But since most adolescents are in some way alienated from their world, the causes and effects of being a misfit are interesting to them, and they read and evaluate the books with enthusiasm. Further, the question, "Why don't these characters fit into their world?" leads the class into good discussions of morality, values, and history that are downright philosophical!

A final suggestion is that a wonderful choice for summer reading to lead into this course, if the school has such a policy, is John Kennedy Toole's *A Confederacy of Dunces.* It is funny and new and therefore palatable to kids on vacation, and it also leads beautifully into the questions and issues of "The Misfit in Literature."

A "Novel" Approach to the Classics Relating Art and Literature

Beverly Baker
New Trier High School, Winnetka, Illinois

You can ignite the interest of the secondary-level English student by assigning a classic work of literature with a novel teaching approach. Rather than explicate the literary work in a formalistic way using the work alone, assign the analysis of a classic along with the analysis of a painting of the student's choice (e.g., *Crime and Punishment* by Fyodor Dostoevski and *Starry Night* by Vincent Van Gogh). The painting, however, must bear some relationship to the classic itself that the student must ultimately defend in a final expository essay. By combining art and literature, the teacher can encourage new and surprising interpretations, developed out of relationships between two ostensibly discrete disciplines.

Students should begin this investigation by asking the same questions of both art forms. The following paragraphs offer guidelines for comparing the two.

What are the themes of both the classic and the painting? Are these themes "universal," relevant to all people? Do the dominating ideas in both works seem similar? Are both works optimistic about the future of humanity? Or do they see humanity as evil? Do you agree with them? Is this theme appropriate for our day and age?

When and where is the painting taking place, and how is this setting similar to that of the classic? What are the physical arrangements in both works? What are the times in which their actions take place? What is the general environment of each? Could the scenes happen elsewhere as well? How important is the setting to both artistic works? Are the settings believable? Do the settings help to create similar moods? Keep in mind that you are tying threads of similarity between one art form and the other.

Are there parallels between or among the characters in both works? How important are they? What do you infer these characters are like emotionally? What are they like spiritually? Are they happy within themselves? Could the characters in both works relate to each other? Are they

11

similar in that they are stereotypical? Is there a common problem they might face? Every successful characterization becomes an example of the universal. Can the characters in both the painting and the classic represent something in relation to the world at large?

A conflict is a struggle between two opposing forces. What are the two opposing forces in both the painting and the classic? Are they significant or trivial? Is there a problem leading up to the conflict in both worlds? Can you resolve the conflicts in both in a similar fashion? Are the conflicts between characters or ideas? Is the conflict in both character against character, character against self, character against society, or character against nature? Would you take the same side in both works?

Every classic and every painting has a tone, an attitude toward its subject matter. What are the tones created by the artist and the author? Are the attitudes serious? playful? ironic? intimate? Would the artist and the author enjoy the company of their characters? Would they consider the characters trustworthy? friendly? What might the tone be toward the environment? Are both works akin in tone?

The mood expresses the attitudes of the characters toward the theme or toward one another. What are the attitudes of the characters? Are their attitudes predictable? Could the characters be friends? What attitude is the reader encouraged to hold toward both the characters and theme of the classic and the painting?

A plot is a series of episodes or actions. Could you make up a plot for the painting that coincides with or is similar to the plot of the classic? Would the characters in each be behaving realistically? rationally? emotionally? Would the two plots have similar endings?

A symbol is something that is itself, yet stands for, or suggests, something else. Are there objects in both the painting and the classic that might stand for some larger idea? Are there meanings on any other level than the literal?

Point of view is the way in which the artistic expression is presented by the painter and the writer. Every time the point of view changes, the message changes. The point of view results from the artist's consciousness. Are the points of view in these two works similar? If so, how? Draw parallels. Draw relationships.

What is the title of each work of art? Could you interchange the titles and still be consistent with the form and content of each work? Are the works similar although the titles are not? Could you give the same title to both works?

After studying the classic and the painting, and answering the questions listed previously, the students should write well-developed multi-paragraph expository essays defending the choice of their particular paintings, and revealing some parallel or similarity to the classic under study.

Incorporating the analysis of a painting into the analysis of a classic is a fresh approach that will not only stimulate your students, but will also enhance their understanding of the literary work itself. Working on two dimensions simultaneously expands the consciousness of a student who may not see an operative literary element clearly, but may, on the other hand, see a similar element on the visual level. "Of all the passions that possess mankind, / the love of novelty rules most the mind" (Samuel Foote). This approach may be the very novelty that will inspire your students to explore the classics with gusto.

Archetypes in *A Tale of Two Cities*

Margaret B. Fleming
University of Arizona, Tucson

A Tale of Two Cities is one of Charles Dickens's most powerful works. Unfortunately, the typical way of approaching it—focusing on plot, character, and setting—is likely to bring out its weaknesses, rather than its strengths. Students find the plot contrived and the characters lacking in verisimilitude—Lucie Manette too good to be true, Sydney Carton too good to be bad, and Jerry Cruncher and Miss Pross caricatures too gross to be congruent with a serious novel. As for the setting, the two cities, London and Paris, are both so far removed from our students' experience as to be virtually indistinguishable. Nor is this reaction unique to *A Tale of Two Cities*. For a variety of reasons students may find classic novels, particularly those of the nineteenth century, inaccessible or irrelevant.

A more productive way of approaching these novels may be to focus on their paradoxes as expressed through archetypes. Dickens, for example, uses these universal symbols of human experience in *A Tale of Two Cities* to emphasize the cosmic struggle between creative and destructive forces, represented by the French Revolution and on a smaller scale in the lives of individuals. Since archetypes derive from the most fundamental of human experiences—natural cycles, family relationships, colors, concepts of good and evil—students should, after some practice, be able to give concrete representations or images their symbolic significance. For example, the cycle of a day may represent a human life, from the morning of youth to the sleep of death; fire may stand for warmth, both physical and emotional; the hand for action; a road for the journey of life; water for purification; and so on. Succinct explanations of the archetypal approach to literature are provided by Wilfred Guerin et al. in *A Handbook of Critical Approaches to Literature* (New York: Harper & Row, 1979) and Peter Stillman in *Introduction to Myth* (Rochelle Park, N.J.: Hayden, 1977); Northrop Frye's *Anatomy of Criticism* (New York: Atheneum, 1966) is an extended treatment.

One way to begin the study of these archetypes in *A Tale of Two*

Cities is to discover the ways in which paradox and contradiction are expressed. The tension set up by the opening lines, "It was the best of times, it was the worst of times," pervades the novel; before going any further in the book, a teacher might ask a class to consider, either orally or in writing, the ways in which our own period of history is the best of times, the worst of times. Then the historical allusions Dickens uses can point up similarities. Louis XVI and Marie Antoinette, George III and Charlotte, can be compared with present-day world rulers. Mrs. Joanna Southcott, who claims revelations, typifies the rise of religious cults in all ages. The inevitability of the Revolution, personified in the Farmer and the Woodman, can easily be seen to resemble current large-scale political movements. A thorough discussion along these lines should help students to see the universality, as well as the uniqueness, of the events Dickens is about to recount, and also to see the paradoxical nature of many memorable experiences, both historical and personal.

Three pairs of archetypes express particularly well the paradoxes and contrasts that form the novel's fabric. They are embodied in character, in imagery, and in plot.

The Great Mother and the Terrible Mother are complementary female archetypes. The first is a nurturer, the second a destroyer, often taking the form of a witch or sorceress. Lucie may be more believable if she is seen as a Great Mother figure. She is all things to all men, functioning superbly as daughter, wife, mother, and friend. Madame Defarge is her counterpart, the Terrible Mother; in her the same relationships are distorted by hatred, and she becomes a force for evil rather than good.

The corresponding contrasts in the male characters are usually seen in the Hero and the Villain, archetypes familiar from Western movies. In Charles Darnay and Sydney Carton, however, there is a different kind of contrast, that between the hero and his alter ego. Charles is what Sydney might have been, and vice versa. Students can be asked who the hero of this novel is, and who the villain, or even if there is one. They can also be asked to identify other pairs of opposing characters and to discuss how they function. Do any of them seem to be types rather than realistic characters? If so, what human traits do they represent? Most characters in this novel are not, strictly speaking, archetypes, but many lack the kind of verisimilitude typical of contemporary literature and function better as symbols than as realistic characters.

Dickens's imagery is frequently archetypal. One technique he uses to express paradox is to link conflicting archetypes in clusters. The most frequent such cluster is *blood-wine-red-sun*. Remembering that archetypes have universal, or nearly universal, significance, students can be led to discover their symbolism by brainstorming associations with the concrete terms. A teacher could begin by asking students what words they think of in connection with "blood" and "sun." A typical list might read as follows:

Blood	*Sun*
death	day
violence	light
passion	warmth
murder	health
crime	well-being
guilt	prosperity
heredity	wholeness
wine	brightness
salvation	

It is easy to see that the most common associations of "blood" have to do with negative and destructive human impulses (even "salvation" is linked with a deed of extreme violence). The associations of "sun," on the other hand, are positive and creative. Extending the sun symbolism to "rising sun" and "setting sun" provides a further contrast:

Rising Sun	*Setting Sun*
dawn	darkness
hope	old age
youth	cold
new beginning	death
birth	night
light	end
warmth	despair

At many significant points throughout the novel blood is linked with the sun—either the rising or the setting sun—through the color red, which is common to both. Blood is also linked to wine through its color and through its significance in Christian theology. (Interested students might be encouraged to pursue this connection also.) As they read the novel, students can be instructed to look for these clusters of images and to discuss their significance.

In book 2, chapter 8, "Monseigneur in the Country," there is this passage:

> The sunset struck so brilliantly into the traveling carriage when it gained the hill-top, that its occupant was steeped in crimson. "It will die out," said Monsieur the Marquis, glancing at his hands, "directly."

In effect, the sun was so low that it dipped at that moment. When the heavy drag had been adjusted to the wheel, and the carriage slid down hill, with a cinderous smell, in a cloud of dust, the red glow departed quickly; the sun and the Marquis going down together, there was no glow left when the drag was taken off.[1]

Questions that might be asked are

What is significant about the color of the Marquis's hands? Does this remind you of any other well-known literary or historical incidents?

What is meant by "the sun and the Marquis going down together"?

How will the crimson die out from the Marquis's hands?

Does the cinderous smell have any other than literal significance?

Other passages that invite this kind of close reading and discussion follow. Words with archetypal significance have been italicized.

Lighter and *lighter,* until at last the *sun* touched the tops of the still trees, and poured its radiance over the hill. In the *glow,* the *water* of the chateau fountain seemed to turn to *blood,* and the stone faces *crimsoned* ("The Gorgon's Head," p. 157).

The chateau awoke later. . . . First the lonely boar-spears and knives of the chase had been *reddened as of old;* then had *gleamed* trenchant in the *morning sunshine* (p. 158).

The great grindstone, Earth, had turned when Mr. Lorry looked out again, and the *sun* was *red* on the court-yard. But, the lesser grindstone stood alone there in the calm *morning* air, with a *red* upon it that the *sun* had never given, and would never take away ("The Grindstone," p. 293).

Blood is also linked with wine in many places, with symbolic significance. In book 1, chapter 5, "The Wine-Shop," when a cask of wine is spilled in the street and Gaspard scrawls the word *blood* on the wall, this comment follows: "The time was to come when *that wine* too would be spilled on the streetstones, and when the *stain* of it would be *red* upon many there" (p. 61). This motif is taken up again much later in the chapter "Echoing Footsteps." These are

the loudly echoing footsteps of Saint Antoine, . . . headlong, mad, and dangerous; and in the years so long after the *breaking of the cask* at Defarge's wine-shop door, they are not easily *purified* when once *stained red* (p. 250).

A similar association occurs near the end of the book, when Sydney fills a glass with brandy (students might want to discover the connection between wine and brandy) and pours it out upon the hearth, prefiguring his sacrifice and linking the blood-sun imagery with death and resurrection.

Death and resurrection are stages in the narrative of the quest of the hero. This narrative pattern is so widespread that it is sometimes known as the *monomyth.* In *Mythology: The Voyage of the Hero* (New York: Harper & Row, 1980), David Adams Leeming identifies the following stages and illustrates them with examples drawn from the literature, religion, and folklore of widely divergent cultures:

Miraculous birth

Early signs of greatness

Period of withdrawal or preparation

Quest, voyage, or mission

Death as scapegoat

Descent into the underworld

Resurrection

Atonement and apotheosis

Other authorities divide the pattern into more or fewer stages, but the essential outline is the same. Not all stages occur in all such hero narratives, although many include most of them, at least in embryo. The Christian significance of death and resurrection will be familiar to many students, and this is what Dickens emphasizes, but students can be led to see the universal symbolism by brainstorming their associations with these words:

Death	*Resurrection*
grave	joy
burial	hope
sleep	salvation
night	life
dark	immortality
loss	rebirth
winter	spring

The contrasts here are clear enough, and yet these concepts are dependent on each other. There can be no death without life, no resurrection without death. Dickens, in *A Tale of Two Cities,* makes extensive use of images that draw on the two concepts and their interdependence.

Book 1 of the novel, "Recalled to Life," develops the extended metaphor of a man's being dug out of a grave. Dr. Manette's release from the Bastille is a recall to life both for him, as he escapes from the living death of incarceration, and for his daughter Lucie, to whom he has been dead all her life. Before the reader knows anything of Dr. Manette's history, his recovery is foreshadowed, first by the cryptic message, "recalled to life," and then by the crowded and incoherent images of Mr. Lorry's dream:

> There was another current of impression that never ceased to run, all through the night. He was on his way to dig someone out of a grave (p. 46).

> "Buried how long?". . .
> "Almost eighteen years.". . .
> "You know that you are recalled to life?"
> "They tell me so."
> "I hope you care to live."
> "I can't say." (pp. 46-47)

> After much imaginary discourse, the passenger in his fancy would dig and dig, dig—now with a spade, now with a great key, now with his hands—to dig this wretched creature out (p. 47).

Sleep is of course an archetype for death, and the dream mechanism itself may be seen as a kind of digging out of the subconscious mind the ideas, hopes, and fears buried there. Indeed, Dickens, at the very beginning of the chapter "The Night Shadows," makes a point of "the wonderful fact . . . that every human creature is constituted to be that profound secret and mystery to every other," closing this paragraph of meditation by asking,

> In any of the *burial-places* of this city through which I pass, is there a *sleeper* more inscrutable than its busy inhabitants are, in their innermost personality, to me, or than I am to them? (p. 44; italics mine)

Later, as Mr. Lorry sits before the coffee-room fire at the inn, his mind is "busily digging, digging, digging, in the live red coals" (p. 51). When he goes to meet Lucie, his perception of her room betrays his preoccupation:

> It was a large, *dark* room, furnished in a *funereal* manner with *black* horsehair, and loaded with heavy *dark* tables. These had been oiled and oiled until the two tall candles on the table in the middle of the room were gloomily reflected on every leaf; as if THEY were *buried,* in deep *graves* of *black* mahogany, and no *light* to speak of could be expected from them until they were *dug out* (pp. 51-52).

The motif persists (or is this pushing it too far?) as Lucie is overcome by Mr. Lorry's news and has to be "recalled to life" by Miss Pross.

The culmination of the extended metaphor comes at the end of part 1 when Dr. Manette, "the buried man who had been dug out," is on his way home in a stagecoach opposite Mr. Lorry, who recalls his earlier dream with its recurrent question, "I hope you care to be recalled to life?" Dr. Manette's answer is the same, but unspoken. At this point he literally "can't say."

The motif "recalled to life" recurs periodically throughout the rest of the book. After Charles's trial for treason, it is underlined by Jerry Cruncher, who is to bear the message "Acquitted." "'If you had sent the message "recalled to life" again,' muttered Jerry, as he turned, 'I should have known what you meant, this time'" (p. 109). Charles is indeed recalled to life from almost certain death by Sydney's fortuitous notice of the resemblance between them, a prefiguring of the later occasion when he makes use of the resemblance to recall Charles to life for Lucie. Charles is actually recalled to life three times, the first by being acquitted of treason against England, the second by being acquitted of a similar crime against the French Republic through the efforts of Dr. Manette, and the third by being saved from the guillotine by Sydney.

But others too are recalled to life. A teacher might ask a class, "How many characters in this novel are recalled to life, and in what sense?" Students can usually name the following: Miss Pross's long-lost brother Solomon, dead to her for many years, who turns up in Paris as the spy and turncoat John Barsad; Roger Cly, his partner in crime, whose false funeral Jerry Cruncher has attended, and who is "recalled to life" by Jerry's information about his empty coffin; and Jerry himself, who in his moonlighting occupation of digging up graves and selling the bodies for medical experiments is a "resurrection-man." Some answers will be more far-fetched, but not without justification: the peasants in France are recalled to life after they revolt; Sydney is recalled to life when Charles and Lucie name their next child after him, and the boy grows up to follow Sydney's profession; not only Charles, but Lucie, her daughter, Jerry Cruncher, and Miss Pross are recalled to life by escaping from France.

Students may have difficulty in seeing that Sydney is recalled to life, since he actually dies. Yet his death is the climax of the death-resurrection theme. Like other heroes of the quest tradition, he becomes a scapegoat, sacrificing himself that others may live. After discussion, students should be able to see that his death is truly a resurrection. All through the fateful night before Charles's third and last trial, as Sydney walks the streets of Paris, preparing himself for what he must do, he repeats over and over the words of the burial service: "I am the resurrection and the life, saith the Lord: he that believeth in me, though he were dead, yet shall he live; and whosoever liveth and believeth in me, shall never die" (p. 343). At this point Sydney's likeness to the quest hero is most pronounced. The stages of preparation, mission, death, descent into hell, and resurrection can all be traced symbolically in the archetypal images of the following description:

> The *night* wore out; and as he stood upon the bridge listening to the *water* as it splashed the river-walls of the Island of Paris, where the picturesque confusion of houses and cathedral shone *bright* in the *light* of the moon, the *day* came *coldly*, looking like a *dead* face out of the sky. Then, the *night*, with the moon and the stars, turned *pale* and *died*, and for a little while it seemed as if Creation were delivered over to *Death's Dominion*.
>
> But the glorious *sun, rising*, seemed to strike those words, that burden of the *night*, straight and *warm to his heart* in its long *bright* rays. And looking along them, with reverently shaded eyes, a *bridge of light* appeared to span the air between him and the *sun*, while the *river sparkled* under it (pp. 343-344; italics mine).

Students can be asked to speculate upon the significance of this profusion of archetypes:

Why is the cathedral "bright in the light of the moon"?

Why does the day come "coldly"?

What words does the sun seem to strike? What does this mean? What is implied by "warm to his heart"?

What is the significance of the bridge of light? The sparkling river?

To what kind of life is Sydney recalled? From what kind of death?

The greatness of *A Tale of Two Cities* and other classic novels lies in the emotional intensity of the experiences they portray. This intensity is underlined by the use of archetypes, symbols that reach deep into the collective unconscious of all humanity. Discovering their significance can greatly add to readers' appreciation of any work.

Note

1. Charles Dickens, *A Tale of Two Cities* (New York: Penguin, 1982), 144. Subsequent page references are to this edition.

"Huckstering" the Classics

Constance Bowman Cylkowski
Winchester School, Northville, Michigan

What a splendid idea Greg Matthews had when he wrote his sequel to the *Adventures of Huckleberry Finn! The Further Adventures of Huckleberry Finn,* recently published by Crown (New York, 1983), gives the classroom teacher a perfect opportunity to develop students' interest in reading Mark Twain's story not just for enjoyment, but also for the challenge of predicting the form and direction a successful "follow-up" story could take. A study of *Huckleberry Finn* and its 1983 sequel can inspire enthusiastic reading, discussion, and writing in high-school or college students. This study could introduce students to a creative way of reading the classics and writing about them.

In introducing any classic work, the teacher can ask: What is there about this story that could inspire a present-day author to write a sequel? About *Huckleberry Finn* in particular, a teacher can inquire: What elements are there in Twain's tale that would make an author of today think that another story about Huck could be appealing and successful in our times? The search for an answer to these questions can motivate students to read a classic with a sense of inquiry and investigation. As the first step in a reading and writing unit, their search will lead them to discover the universality of human experience reflected in all good literature.

As a second step, students can be directed to discuss and write about the parallels they find in the classics to their own or their peers' experience. They can certainly empathize with Huck's attempts to understand and deal with the adult world—from Miss Watson, who keeps "pecking" at him, to the king and the duke, who try to con everyone they meet. Students will find topics such as parental alcoholism and racism effectively delineated by Twain and still prevalent today, as well as the struggle of individuals like Huck and Jim when they face these problems.

Teachers must be careful, though, in guiding students to express their thoughts about the classics, that their attention is focused on the literature itself, and that discussion or writing is always based on the story and not merely on topics that might spring from their reading of the story. For instance, teachers should not encourage comments or papers dealing with racism in our contemporary society merely because Twain presents that evil in his book. Rather, students should be motivated to discover and then relate how effectively the author portrays character, depicts setting, and constructs a plot to reflect the customs and mores of his society and influence the thoughts and feelings of his readers.

An analysis of how the author uses character, setting, and plot to produce an effective and enduring story can lead to a third step in a unit of study of the classics. The teacher can ask students to imagine what a sequel to the classic they have just read would be like. What characters would be best included or excluded? Where would the new story be likely to take place? What events would make the new plot plausible in light of the way the characters felt and acted in the original story? These points offer rich material for analytical discussion and writing, and lead the way, if teacher and student wish, to the culmination of the unit in a burst of creative writing—"O.K. We've talked about what a sequel should or could be like; now write the first chapter of *your* follow-up story!"

Using *Huckleberry Finn* as the first story in a study of the classics affords the opportunity to compare the imaginary sequel that the students project in their discussion or writing with the sequel that Greg Matthews has actually written. This unit on the classics could continue with the reading of *The Further Adventures of Huckleberry Finn* and an analysis of this contemporary work using the same focal points of character, setting, and plot as were used in analyzing Twain's *Huckleberry Finn*. Students will better understand the relevance and validity of studying the classics after completing this unit on Mark Twain's book and its sequel. They will be motivated to read other classics, analyze and discuss them, and perhaps write successful sequels of their own!

Aristotle and the Declaration of Independence

Clyde A. Moneyhun
Nagoya International College, Nagoya, Japan

Marvin D. Diogenes
University of Arizona, Tucson

The purpose of this integrated series of readings, classroom discussions, and writing assignments is to give fairly unsophisticated college students an understanding of the Declaration of Independence as an exemplary piece of rhetoric. The skills of analysis they learn will enable them to examine the rhetorical strategies of any short piece of persuasive political rhetoric. Ultimately, the students should see the clear rhetorical relationships between *what* is said, *how* it is said, *by* whom, and *to* whom. In this way they may come to perceive texts as we would like them to: not as cold, dead artifacts from the past, but as a living exchange of thoughts and feelings between real human beings.

The foundation for this two-to-three-week study unit is a careful discussion of the first twenty or so pages of Aristotle's *Rhetoric* (book 1, chapters 1-3). While the archaic style of most translations causes trouble for a few students, the material is really quite clear, concise, and accessible. The Lane Cooper translation (which we recommend) even includes interspersed explanations to clarify Aristotle's ideas. For a brief summary of this material and its relation to the Declaration, see the Appendix, which serves as an answer guide to the homework questions. The bibliography contains several other background sources on the subject.

Homework Assignment #1: Read in Aristotle's *Rhetoric* book 1, chapter 1 and the beginning of chapter 2 (about ten pages). Answer the following questions in a paragraph or two: What is Aristotle's special definition of the word *rhetoric?* In what ways does Aristotle think rhetoric is useful? Against what criticisms does he defend it?

Classroom Discussion #1: Clarify and extend Aristotle's meaning with a discussion based on the questions of the homework assignment and also the following: What is the *dictionary* definition of the word *rhetoric?*

How does it differ from Aristotle's? What about the popular definition of rhetoric as "empty, flowery speech"? What would Aristotle say about that? What is *not* rhetoric, according to Aristotle? How can rhetoric be misused? Can you think of any current examples? (Teachers might find it useful to bring in some examples from the morning paper.) In view of such misuse, does Aristotle's defense of the usefulness of rhetoric satisfy you?

Homework Assignment #2: Read the rest of chapter 2 and also chapter 3. Answer the following questions in a paragraph or two: What does Aristotle mean by the distinction between "artistic" and "non-artistic" means of persuasion? What are his three major "artistic" means of persuasion? What kinds of logical proofs are part of a rhetorical argument?

Classroom Discussion #2: Begin by clarifying Aristotle's three "kinds" of rhetoric and their characteristic "aims," material covered in chapter 3 but not part of the homework assignment. Continue through the homework questions, and use the last one to clarify Aristotle's concept of "enthymeme." With the help of the students' suggestions, construct several enthymemes on the board and use them to explain how enthymemes in general function. (Again, teachers might also come prepared with enthymemes from current events.)

Homework Assignment #3: Write a half dozen enthymemes.

Classroom Discussion #3: Have the students write what they consider their best enthymemes on the board. Ask the class as a whole to analyze them by means of the following criteria: Are they structured as enthymemes? Are the premises true, or acceptable enough to stand up to criticism? Does the conclusion follow logically from the premises?

Homework Assignment #4: Read the Declaration of Independence. Make notes on any of the rhetorical elements discussed so far that you can see in the Declaration. Refer to your homework assignments and class notes to refresh your memory.

Classroom Discussion #4: Analyze the rhetoric of the Declaration of Independence with a discussion based on the following questions, referring always to specific passages in the text itself for answers:

1. What "kind" of rhetoric is the Declaration of Independence? How would Aristotle classify it? What are the "aims" of the Declaration?

2. Who is the audience, as well as you can guess from indications in the text? What role does the audience play? What is the purpose of defining the audience in this way?

3. Who is the speaker? That is, who is doing the "declaring"? What "tone of voice" or "personality" does the speaker have? How does it serve the speaker's purpose to adopt such a tone of voice?

4. What is the overall organization of the Declaration? What is its logical structure? What purpose does this structure serve?

5. How do the choice of audience, tone of voice, and logical structure work together?

6. What is the enthymeme in paragraph 2 of the text? (As students answer, write it on the board for easy reference.) How do the items on the list of grievances (which follows paragraph 2) grow out of the terms of the enthymeme? (How are they violations of the basic rights asserted in the enthymeme?) Why is the conclusion of the enthymeme so radical and so dangerous that Benjamin Franklin said as he signed his name to the Declaration, "Well, now we must all hang together, or we will surely hang separately"?

The discussion might end with a sketch of King George III's treatment of the colonies and his reaction to their declaration of rebellion.

Homework Assignment #5: Imagine that you are King George III. Write a brief reply to the assertions in paragraph 2 of the Declaration of Independence. Before you write, determine what audience you're writing to and what tone of voice you intend to use; explain your choices in a paragraph or two. Frame your reply as a "counter-enthymeme" that contradicts the Declaration's enthymeme point by point and then reaches a conclusion opposite to that of the Declaration.

A follow-up discussion to this last assignment might examine how the enthymeme expressed in paragraph 2 of the Declaration of Independence gave rise to many other basic American principles. In what other areas of American life and thought do we see these ideas? How might our implicit belief in these principles lead to misunderstandings between Americans and other nationalities?

This series of readings, discussions, and writing assignments is integrated in the sense that a controlled number of rhetorical elements are introduced, explained, and used to analyze a text. Thus the material students learn in homework assignments 1 and 2 comes back and is useful to them during classroom discussion 4. Students get practice in identifying the set of rhetorical elements they have learned in homework assignment 4 and in actually using them in homework assignments 3 and 5. (The Appendix will further clarify the integral relationship between the Aristotle material and the Declaration itself.)

A study unit such as this one can be a starting point for many others. Particularly appropriate texts for rhetorical study and discussion following the Declaration would be other great pieces of American political rhetoric, such as the Constitution (especially the Preamble), Lincoln's Gettysburg Address (analyzed by Lane Cooper in his introduction to *The Rhetoric of Aristotle*), Thoreau's *Civil Disobedience* or "Plea for Captain John Brown," and Martin Luther King's "Letter from the Birmingham Jail." Homework assignments and classroom discussions should, like the ones we've sketched, stress the relationship between the ideas in the texts and the rhetoric with which the ideas are made effective. Above all, students should be encouraged to produce rhetoric of their own to fit the requirements of specific situations.

Appendix

Summary of Aristotle's Rhetoric, *Book 1, Chapters 1–3*

Aristotle defines *rhetoric* as "the ability to discover all the available means of persuasion in a given situation." The rest of the *Rhetoric* can be seen as a clarification of what is meant by "discovery" and "means of persuasion." Aristotle thinks that rhetoric is useful in four major ways:

1. We can use it to argue for what we know to be true and right, and thus prevent the triumph of fraud and injustice.

2. While we may know that something is true, we may not be believed unless we can phrase it in such a way that it also *appears* to be true and plausible to an audience; this is one thing rhetoric enables us to do.

3. It helps us to see both sides of an argument, to weigh our opponent's ideas, to be fair and logical.

4. It helps us defend ourselves against those who would take advantage of us through trickery and deceit.

To the criticism that rhetoric can be misused to deceive the listener, Aristotle replies that "the same charge can be brought against all good things. . . . Rightly employed, they work the greatest blessings; and wrongly employed, they work the utmost harm." In other words, rhetoric is merely a tool; if it is misused, the fault lies with the person who used the tool, not with the tool itself.

When Aristotle uses the terms "artistic" and "non-artistic" for means of persuasion, he is talking about those means of persuasion that are "of the art" and "not of the art" of rhetoric. The non-artistic means of persuasion or "proofs" are later (book 1, chapter 15) enumerated: laws, witnesses, contracts, tortures, and oaths. Why they are "not of the art" of rhetoric becomes clearer when Aristotle defines the three major "artistic" means of persuasion:

1. The kind of persuasion produced through an audience's perception of the character (or *ethos*) of the speaker.

2. The kind of persuasion a speaker uses to produce a certain attitude, state of mind, or emotional state in the audience *(pathos)*.

3. The kind of persuasion produced through logical arguments *(logos)*. By "logical argument" Aristotle means the two major ways of arguing, through induction (basing conclusions on examples) or through deduction

(basing conclusions on a series of "general truths"). This last method of argument requires the construction of "enthymemes," or "rhetorical syllogisms."

Aristotle deals with enthymemes in more detail in book 2, chapters 22–25. They may be defined as "syllogisms of everyday life," or syllogisms that don't need to be mathematically airtight like those of formal logic. The premises need to be true only insofar as the audience addressed *believes* they are true; premises that the audience accepts as a matter of course may even be omitted.

Aristotle defines three major kinds of rhetoric: deliberative (or legislative), forensic (or legal), and ceremonial. Deliberative discourse exhorts or dissuades the audience concerning future action, and its aim is to recommend the most expedient means by which the audience may achieve its ends. Forensic discourse accuses or defends a person concerning past actions, and its aim is justice. Ceremonial discourse praises or blames a person for present actions, and its aim is to honor or dishonor the person.

Summary of the Rhetoric of the Declaration of Independence

The Declaration contains elements of all three of Aristotle's kinds of rhetoric. In that it is a personal attack on the character of the king, it is ceremonial discourse. In that it puts him on trial with a long series of accusations, finding him guilty of tyranny, it is forensic discourse. In that it defines freedom as the end the audience desires, and recommends revolution as the most expedient (indeed, the only) means of achieving that end, it is deliberative.

The audience is cast in the role of judge. This is made explicit in the way the speaker says he wants to "let Facts be submitted to a candid World," and by the appeal in the last paragraph to "the Supreme Judge of the World."

The speaker's voice is an ingenious combination of calm reasonableness and righteous indignation, humility and moral rectitude, reluctance to rebel and decisiveness. Above all, the voice claims to speak as a representative of a united American people, to speak by their authority and in their interests.

The arrangement of points in the Declaration is also quite effective. The enthymeme is stated in general, philosophical terms, ending in the radical conclusion that under certain conditions, people have the right to overthrow their government. The theoretical conditions are made specific to the case of the colonies in the end of the paragraph, and the conclusion repeated. Nearly every grievance may be traced directly back to the terms of the original enthymeme. The Declaration ends with a repetition of the colonists' intentions.

References

Aristotle. *The Rhetoric of Aristotle,* trans. Lane Cooper. Englewood Cliffs, N. J.: Prentice-Hall, 1960.
Cooper's introduction is very useful, as are his annotations of Aristotle.

Corbett, Edward P. J. *Classical Rhetoric for the Modern Student.* New York: Oxford University Press, 1971.
This is the classic "update" of Aristotle, and includes essays for analysis, many accompanied by analyses of the Aristotelian rhetoric they contain.

Gage, John T. "Teaching the Enthymeme: Invention and Arrangement." *Rhetoric Review* 2, no. 1 (Sept. 1983): 38-50.
This article is distinguished by the many practical techniques it offers to show students how to use enthymemes as tools of invention in their own writing.

Ginsburg, Robert, ed. *A Casebook on the Declaration of Independence.* New York: Thomas Y. Crowell Company, 1967.
This excellent source book contains the text of the Declaration and many fine essays, including contemporary commentaries and replies, political and philosophical assessments, and a very good rhetorical analysis by the editor.

Jacobus, Lee A. *A World of Ideas.* New York: St. Martin's Press, 1983.
The introduction ("Writing About Ideas: An Introduction to Rhetoric") shows students how to approach texts rhetorically, and each essay in the reader is prefaced by a short rhetorical analysis.

2 The Literature-Writing Connection

Writing Allegories: A Route to the Classics

Wanda Burzycki
Rincon Valley Junior High, Santa Rosa, California

Embarking on the *Odyssey* with a class of ninth-graders well grounded in study skills, research papers, and career education was not going to be easy, I realized upon my return from a semester's leave of absence. I sensed their "show *me*, new teacher" attitudes and doubted that they'd explore Homer's world to the depths I intended, and I knew lectures explaining and defending classical literature would meet more skepticism. We needed to know each other before we attempted imaginary realms, and they needed a personal journey before they could join Odysseus. So I launched them full sail, assigning them to write the stories of their lives in allegorical form, and discovered with them a project which not only carried us smoothly through the *Odyssey* but led us further into literature than I'd ever expected.

"No, an allegory is not a medieval monster with scaly wings and dragon breath," I explained over the mild tumult which greeted this "getting to know you" assignment. I gave them a dictionary definition: "a literary, dramatic, or pictorial representation, the apparent or superficial sense of which both parallels and illustrates a deeper sense" (*The American Heritage Dictionary*, 1975); described its prevalence in classic and even contemporary works; and stood ready with examples. I was confident, actually, that the concept would eventually appeal to them. Adolescents tend toward oblique and exaggerated forms of expression anyway, using metaphor-laden slang and appreciating innuendo, symbolism, and multiple meanings. According to Piaget and other researchers[1] as adolescents attain the level of formal operations, which includes the ability to comprehend and express conceptual metaphors, they naturally explore their new capacities. This is reflected in some of the literature they choose— fantasy and science fiction, in which a theme or moral is expressed in more remote yet somehow more acceptable terms (C. S. Lewis comes to mind). And during what period but adolescence are both the desire and the fear that someone else will know one so evident? Allegory, with all its

33

enigmatic imagery, fulfills their need for expression well. I continued my explanation.

Together we recalled the remnants of Greek mythology from their eighth-grade studies, listing gods and heroes and the qualities each embodied. (This review also helped prepare them for the approaching *Odyssey*.) I then asked them to skip a number of centuries and describe the Middle Ages. Since they were currently immersed in that period in their history classes, they had much to share about cruel monarchs, downtrodden peasants, and dismal living conditions. We discussed the influence of the Roman Catholic church, and I told them how morality plays used characters to represent good, evil, and humankind to convey deeper lessons in a form accessible to the peasants. We moved on to the Renaissance, and I pulled out a print of Botticelli's *Birth of Venus*. "Does this look like a religious painting?" I asked, and produced more Renaissance prints of sensual and beautiful bodies. We concluded that the allegorical representations justified the figures. I read a few passages from Dante's *Inferno* to illustrate how he used the form to imply his political and theological opinions, and then I leaped forward a few more centuries to discuss Swift's *Gulliver's Travels*. I tied in the present with one of Art Hoppe's columns from the *San Francisco Chronicle,* which several of the students recalled, and finally someone brought up Norton Juster's *Phantom Tollbooth*. With this, we were on our way.

Intrigued, they felt satisfied about the meaning of "allegory" but still intimidated by the word *life*. I comforted them with a sheet listing the procedure for writing their stories and then demonstrated the process with my own allegory. (Part of my enthusiasm for the whole project had stemmed from the sense of artfulness and self-indulgence I felt putting my story together.)

"First you have to make a timeline so you can actually see the life you're dealing with," I said, stretching out a long line of chalk on the board. "Luckily, yours will only be half as long as mine." I outlined my mathematical calculations to determine a midpoint and the approximate lengths of my year-segments. To help the students work out their own timelines, I borrowed a student's life and went through each step with them. ("Let's see, 1982 minus 1967 equals . . . and half of that is . . . and if the line is ten inches long . . .") Math flourished across the curriculum that day.

Once everyone had drawn and divided the lines, I began the next step—indicating where "significant" events fall on the line. After designating my birthdate (more math as they calculated my age), I wrote in those events I wished to share—graduations, changes of schools and residences, travels. We brainstormed other events to aid those people who felt that "nothing important" had occurred in their short lives. This list included acquisitions of new siblings and/or parents, divorce, meeting and losing best friends, involvement in sports or other groups; in turn, these sparked more personal recollections. As the students began marking in these events, the exchange of personal experiences grew, and the discussion among students and even with me reached further than I'd expected.

The most difficult step involved the transposition of the abstract life into a concrete theme for the allegory. I distributed copies of my finished timeline, map, and story (I'd chosen a simple car-trip motif) to show how someone who is not Dante actually can write an allegory. I began: "Looking back on it now, I realize I've been traveling on this road for a long time. The road has brought me my share of adventures, and I've survived so far, but I'm always driving, wondering what's up ahead. Some kind of change is always guaranteed. I am told my first experiences occurred along country roads . . ." The students surprised me with their interest and appreciated my imagery as I pointed out how I had literally "bent" my timeline and drawn in the same metaphors (mountains, straight highways) I had used in my writing. Soon they came up with many ideas for allegorical themes, and we listed them—backpacking trips, various sports, rocket flights, and others which the students kept for themselves. Most chose a concept with which they were familiar, and they were eager to start.

Though I required that they turn in both a written account and a visual representation of their allegories, I did not dictate which they had to complete first during the allotted time for the rough drafts. While I had found it easier to write first, other people like to use the visual concept to organize and guide the writing. Giving them the option allowed for more choice in the "right/left brain" approach. Either way, once the students started, I noticed what pleasure they took in creating consistent and meaningful metaphors—and though some may have been clichéd, since the whole process was new to them I did not push for further originality.

Since I did not feel the class was ready to work in response groups, especially with work of such a personal nature, I had them respond in pairs. I asked them to look for parallel structure and consistency, and I gave examples of mixed metaphors. We also focused on possibilities for endings; many students had difficulty concluding the stories of their lives when obviously the stories continued in reality. Devising sentences to express the writer's general outlook about the future took many examples and reworkings, but the class generally picked up the tone. Again, because the approach to life was so different for them, I did not cover avoiding trite conclusions, though this might be appropriate with a more sophisticated class. Later we worked with parallelism in verb tense and sentence structure, and students applied this during the editing sessions.

They turned in their final drafts and pictures to me for grading and final proofreading. I evaluated the allegories mainly on overall structure and organization (generally chronological), use of detail, parallelism, and originality, and I graded the illustrations on effort and parallelism with the written account, not artistic ability. Upon receipt of the graded work, students recopied the drafts and drawings as necessary and then we posted them all in class, thus solving my bulletin-board problem. Suddenly the room was filled with realms of experiences to explore.

Because these allegories dealt with such personal material, I did not ask students to evaluate the finished works, but they did demonstrate much appreciation, support, and delight in their own creations. I found many of the allegories very touching; in the guise of their metaphors, students had expressed many feelings (rebellion, love, grief), and those who cared could read their meanings. One boy pictured his life as a soccer game, marking out penalties (divorce), team players (little sister, step-mother), and goals (graduation from ninth grade). A usually reserved girl described in detail her flight through space, where her parents kept radioing in new commands and chastising her for being off course. Another girl depicted the rapids and smooth curves she encountered on a river-rafting trip, explaining how her parents and her best friend saved her from drowning. Humor and poignancy intertwined, and the students and I realized how the use of this kind of imagery had freed and extended their ideas.

My initial objectives had been accomplished: students dropped their skepticism about expressive writing (and me), and their imaginations, now pliant with use, were ready to follow Homer. Beyond that, though, they'd experienced the integration of disciplines (art, history, math, even a little geography, science, and P.E. in some of the stories) and the cooperation of both the cognitive and affective domains of thought. Finally, as I had hoped, taking on the double vision of a classical writer of allegory shaped their interpretation of literature throughout the rest of the semester.

While I did not impose a strict allegorical interpretation upon the *Odyssey* (I don't think that is possible), by reminding the students of their allegorical work I helped them appreciate how qualities and values were embodied by the magnificent characters and forces in the tale. Later, we saw how aspects of the *Odyssey* and Greek myths in general have been incorporated in our literature, referring to Tennyson and other writers. Since the students had experienced the power of metaphorical imagery themselves, they demonstrated a willingness to delve deeper for meanings in poetry and classic works rather than just demanding, "Why doesn't he just *say* what he means in plain language?" I did not formally observe how the allegory project had affected their later writing, but the students appeared more receptive when I suggested use of more imagery or figurative language.

It was a relief to find that my teacher's intuition had judged well; not only had this activity meshed the class and me, but it provided a firm base for our approaches to literature and writing through the rest of the year. When students have reflected and traveled within themselves and each other, they are more prepared to set sail with the great writers on new voyages through history and the imagination.

Note

1. Richard M. Billow, "Metaphor: A Review of the Psychological Literature," *Psychological Bulletin* 84 (Jan. 1977): 89-92; and Ellen Winner, "Misunderstanding Metaphor: Cognitive Problem or Pragmatic Problem?" Report for Boston College and Project Zers, 1978.

One Writer to Another: An Approach to "Young Goodman Brown"

Evelyn Farbman
Greater Hartford Community College, Connecticut

In our composition classes we never tire of advising students that the more they read, the better they will eventually write. In my college literature classes I have been acting on the theory that the reverse is also true. Elementary-school teachers have noted that when children start writing their own stories and journals they make rapid progress in decoding and comprehending other texts. Composition teachers have long justified their position at the center of humanities departments by pointing out that expository writing skills are tied to critical thinking, and that in training better writers we are helping students to respond astutely to what they read. So there is a context for my observation that by struggling with their own creative writings, students become more attentive to the craft and resonances of imaginative literature.

"Young Goodman Brown" poses the kinds of problems that respond well to a teaching method based on creative writing. Hawthorne's diction is difficult for my community college students, his theme is troublesome, and if the anthology we're using mentions the terrifying word "symbolism" in presenting the story, many of my students decide at the outset that they'll never "get it." However, two writing projects have helped them enjoy the story and have rewarded me by provoking vigorous classroom discussions.

The first writing assignment is groundwork. I ask the students to get out a piece of paper and to close their eyes. I tell them that they're on the tenth floor of a tall building and have entered the elevator. The door closes and the elevator starts going down. They watch the lights marking the floors: 10, 9, 8, . . . The motion is slow. At the ground floor, the door opens onto a hallway. They walk toward a door and open it to find themselves in the world's most peaceful setting. I ask them to observe the scene in all its detail, keeping their eyes closed throughout. A minute of this silent observation seems like a long time, and after about that long I ask them to open their eyes and write down what they seemed to see, hear, touch, taste, or smell in their imaginary spaces. Even the reluctant students settle down despite disavowals, and everybody writes something. Then I lead them through the exercise again, this time taking them to the world's most terrifying place and asking them to describe it in writing when they open their eyes. The commotion is delightful; everyone has a lot to write for this one and many are sorry to have to part with their papers before they're finished. We all get up and stretch, and in pairs we trade observations about the classroom or the view out the window for a minute to bring us back to our shared reality. For the rest of the class we discuss something else.

After class I read the descriptions (no quibbles about grammar, organization, etc.) and chart the motifs. While each group of students presents its own constellation, one typical chart looks like this:

Category	Peace	Terror
Natural settings	woods, park, beach (4) island, sea (3), lake sun (8), clear sky (7) cool water, dew breezes (2), soft clouds birds (5), squirrels horses (2), butterflies grasses, flowers (6)	forest (2), valley, desert sea night (3), other darkness (4) stormy waves wind (2), dark clouds (2) bees, dogs monsters, snakes bare trees (2), cliffs
Other settings, details	heaven clean room, dining room living room, bedroom candlelight, food (3)	subway, pit, cave, small room highway, hospital, graveyard deathcamp, battleground ax, knife, door, cage
Miscellaneous senses	warmth (3), coolness (2) bird songs (3), rustlings calm voices sunset, blue (3), gold (4) food smells, softness (2)	warmth, burning (2), cold (2) chaotic noises (3), roar crying (2), screams, groans gray (2), black, murky colors sweat, burning flesh smells
Feelings	rich (2), smart, admired floating on sea, on air being in love (3) ecstasy, timelessness (2)	helpless (4), threatened (11) falling (2) being punished, pursued (4) trapped (2), lost (2)
Social setting	lover (2), wedding family (4), children (3) solitude (2)	assailant, demon dead people (2), strangers alone (4), abandoned

Notes: The numbers in parentheses show how many students used the image. No number means that only one student used it. The balance between the two sides of the chart is coincidental.

During the next class, we discuss the chart. (Alternatively, true to the spirit of writing-across-the-curriculum, we might sharpen students' classification skills by presenting them with the raw count of random entries and asking *them* to compose the categories and formulate generalizations.) Students are often surprised to see that other people share what they thought was a unique image, and this moves us toward a discussion of archetypes. Even more lively are the arguments about how "warmth" (for instance) can be part of one person's image of peacefulness, but of another person's image of terror. This leads to questions about what makes a system of images internally coherent as well as evocative of themes beyond itself. Usually I am not the first to use the word "symbolism" and by the time the word surfaces, the concept is fully familiar.

The reading of "Young Goodman Brown" profits in several ways. Many students are intrigued to find Hawthorne's imagery overlapping with their own or with the group's composite—overlapping despite over a century's difference in perspective. Dark forests, snakes, fire, human tumult are all touchstones by now. Some students, through the writing exercise, have caught on to the double vision of figurative language, a skill that opens up their responses to Hawthorne's irony as well as to his allegory. And, finally, everyone is interested in the narrator's question at the end: "Had Goodman Brown fallen asleep in the forest and only dreamed a wild dream of a witch-meeting?" Having gone down their elevators right in the middle of class, they recognize that dream and reality are not polar opposites and that imaginative activity can reach from one mode of consciousness to another. That Goodman Brown's perceptions in the forest that night should alter the rest of his life no longer seems preposterous, though it may continue to be troubling.

There's more to "Young Goodman Brown" than imagery, of course, and once students have something to hold on to, they feel freer to explore the thematic and structural questions. Some of those explorations have yielded better fruit than others, but I have always been pleased with the results of the second creative writing project I offer in our study of "Young Goodman Brown." In my list of suggested topics for midterm essays, I include this:

> Rewrite the ending of "Young Goodman Brown" from the point where Goodman cries "Faith! Faith! . . . look up to heaven, and resist the wicked one." Change the outcome in some significant way but try to maintain the tone, style, and narrative point of view of the original story. When you're through, attach a paragraph or two discussing the problems you encountered and any thoughts about how you've changed the theme.

Since the students can choose to write on some other topic or other work, those who choose this topic are either the ones who have thought carefully about "Young Goodman Brown" or the ones who like to write. Consequently the results often show great care. But even the weaker papers provide excellent opportunities for the class to look one last time at the issues in Hawthorne's story. My students are used to having their papers read by classmates in a peer-critiquing process, and they often work on revisions in small groups, so by midterm most are happy to read their essays to the class. Goodman's changes of destiny at the hands of my students have been by turns hilarious, poignant, nihilistic, bourgeois, outrageous, tragic, and melodramatic, but they have always been fascinating. The writers have confronted difficult questions of craft and emerged with a fresh respect for Hawthorne (often a reversal of a previous attitude). Their classmates have framed criticisms about plausibility, unity, and style. For my part, I have enjoyed sitting in a corner and cheering as they worked together toward the formulation of some ideas as insightful and eloquently expressed as the best I could hope to offer them from the lectern.

Using Writing as a Mode of Learning in Teaching *Beowulf*

Angela A. Rapkin
Manatee Junior College, Bradenton, Florida

At the beginning of my survey course in English literature, I introduce my college students to the idea of writing as a mode of learning. I discuss the concepts implicit in using writing to make meaning or to solve problems creatively, and I offer them the distinction between writer-based and reader-based prose. (A copy of Linda Flower's "Writer-Based Prose: A Cognitive Basis for Problems in Writing" from *College English* 41, no. 1 [Sept. 1979] can be placed on reserve in the library for students wishing to pursue this topic.) If the students in this course have been in any of my previous classes, they are accustomed to the "writing to learn" dittos that I pass out all through the semester as I ask my students to articulate, to work out in writing, their ideas on a variety of subjects and experiences related to the course. For example, in a freshman composition class I am likely to ask students to write out what they learned while doing their first papers. On occasion, several have begun writing with the statement, "I didn't really learn anything from this assignment," and then after exploring the experience ended their essays with, "I guess I did learn something." These students will approach writing as a mode of learning with an established trust that a mode of learning is really what it is, and that their papers will not be criticized and graded.

Students new to the use of writing as a mode of learning may not write as freely as those who have come to trust and enjoy the process. Additional discussion of the topic and perhaps early, simple exercises will help to introduce it.

In English Literature I, one of the first concepts we deal with is the idea of the hero. Because our students probably bring to their reading of *Beowulf,* and later of *Sir Gawain and the Green Knight* and other works involving heroes, certain specific expectations of what a hero is, it is important for them to bring these notions into consciousness and clarify them. This can be done by using writing, even more effectively than in a class discussion, for writing gives everyone the opportunity to work through ideas, not just sit passively as the teacher and only a portion of the class participate.

To facilitate this process, I provide the students with a ditto marked "Writing to Learn," presenting the following directions:

> Before we approach the mythic study of the hero through the Anglo-Saxon poem *Beowulf,* let's clarify our own notions of heroism. Complete the following: To me, a hero is a man or woman who . . .

Halfway down the page I print:

> My definition differs/does not differ from the traditional view of the hero because/in the following ways. First, . . .

This is perhaps more structured than I would like it to be, but it helps the students focus on the topics that will be most important to our discussion.

The exercise has many objectives. In fact, if these objectives were not reinforced in other classes across the curriculum, they would be both too many and too lofty. My aims include the following: offering students an experience in writing to learn; helping students acquire the concept of writing as process; having students use writing to clarify and to solve problems creatively through higher-order reasoning; having students recognize how the self-reflexive process of writing is both a way in itself and an analogue to other ways in which they can approach the task of finding and solving significant problems; and, finally, having students explore and discover ideas of the hero, sorting through those ideas that relate to historical concepts and those that are unique to today's needs.

Once the students have done the writing, then I, seeking common threads, outstanding examples, and unique observations, summarize their points, and to facilitate discussion record them on an overhead transparency. In the first class discussion on these points, I ask specific students to clarify, to elaborate, and to illustrate certain comments they made. It usually takes but one question to begin a lively discussion. No conclusions are drawn, except that Beowulf becomes a clearer figure, and the ideas of myth and archetype become easier to communicate.

Generally during any semester some issue in government, politics, or the arts will surface in our society to make a discussion of the nature of the hero relevant. This semester our government debated the applicability of Martin Luther King's philosophy and life to the definition of the American hero. Should his birthday be a national holiday or not? we asked. The answers revolved around notions of who the American hero is. And how many semesters ago was it that Simon and

Garfunkel bemoaned the loss of the hero when they sang, "Where have you gone, Joe DiMaggio? The nation turns its lonely eyes to you." And that was even before DiMaggio started advertising for Mr. Coffee!

Subsequent papers on the hero—essay tests covering the Anglo-Saxon and medieval periods, or critical papers tracing the evolution of the hero through any number of periods—are ultimately better. They no longer appear to be rough drafts but rather second or third drafts, and, as Elaine Maimon would observe, never finished, but always in process. They are much more enjoyable to read!

In the final analysis, using writing as a mode of learning seeks to foster invention and higher-order reasoning. In my unit on *Beowulf,* this strategy seems to have worked.

Reading, Writing, and the Victorian Novel

Carroll Viera
Tennessee Technological University, Cookeville, Tennessee

Our college students seldom echo the enthusiasm of Victorian readers for novels by writers such as the Brontës, Charles Dickens, George Eliot, and Thomas Hardy. Yet the commercial success of these classics in the nineteenth century suggests their potential appeal for a large reading public, not merely for literary specialists.

One way we can help students develop an appreciation for this fiction is to allow them to read it in the way it was read by the Victorians, who intuitively knew what reader-response critics have recently rediscovered—that meaning is created by a process of interaction between reader and text, not by the text alone. Encouraging this interaction by author intrusions, the novelists engaged in a continual dialogue with the reader, whom they invited to speculate on the directions of the plot and the outcomes of the characters. The conditions of Victorian publication further encouraged this interaction between reader and text in creating meaning, for many novels appeared as installments in periodicals, leaving the reader with a month to ponder forthcoming episodes. By replicating the leisurely Victorian reading process for our students, we can help them to become better readers, teach them to trust their own responses to literature, and expand their appreciation for good fiction. This technique works well with most Victorian novels. I use *The Mill on the Floss* because most of my students come from small communities like St. Ogg's and understand—whether or not they share—the lifestyle and values of the Tullivers.

Book 1 of *Mill* contains an introductory chapter followed by twelve chapters of narrative, which can be grouped nicely into pairs. Chapters 2 and 3 introduce Maggie and begin to develop the contrast between her and Tom. Chapters 4 and 5 prepare for Tom's return and bring him home. Chapters 6 and 7 introduce the Dodson clan and establish Tom's Dodson characteristics. Chapters 8 and 9 develop the Tulliver characteristics and further identify Maggie as a Tulliver struggling to survive in a

Dodson world. Chapters 10 and 11 develop Maggie's struggles in a single episode in which her rashness prompts her to run away. Chapters 12 and 13 link Maggie with her father by giving a further account of the Dodson world and showing Mr. Tulliver's rash rebellion against it.

These groupings allow Book 1 to be assigned over seven class periods, the first period being devoted to the introduction and each remaining period to one pair of chapters. In preparation for these classes, students keep a journal, in which they record a short summary of each reading assignment before the material is discussed. Excluding the descriptive introductory chapter, they complete for each pair of chapters an additional journal entry, in which they speculate on possible directions of the plot, supporting their projections with clues provided by George Eliot.

Both of these writing assignments encourage careful reading: the first requires students to distill from the text what they believe is most important by focusing on *what* the author has said; the second allows them to trace their own responses to the text and to observe *how* the writer engages these responses in order to create meaning. Since the second assignment is speculative rather than factual, students learn that many meanings are often possible and that different readers extract different meanings from the text, discoveries reinforced when journals are read aloud either for the whole class or in small groups. Because this assignment resembles a detective quest, students become eager to read the next chapters to learn whether the author's new clues will confirm or invalidate the previous ones.

A third journal assignment can be added if a curriculum includes formal literary analysis. This assignment requires students to write paragraphs or essays on assigned topics suited to each pair of chapters, such as a character sketch of Maggie constructed from material in chapters 2 and 3 or chapters 10 and 11. After completing several reading assignments, students can also write on topics using material from several chapters, analyzing the Dodson traits, for example, by citing support from chapters 6, 7, 12, and 13. Having already considered each chapter from at least two perspectives in their journals, students can analyze characters and themes with more assurance than they customarily bring to literary topics.

Some, even all, of the journal writing can be completed in class; but if students write at home, class time can be used for comparing various responses and for discussing reasons for the variety. Through exposure to responses that differ from their own, students learn to strengthen their own interpretations by amassing more persuasive support, to reject interpretations that have been carelessly conceived, and to tolerate ambiguity when more than one interpretation can be supported (an especially valuable lesson for students trained to look for *the* meaning of a work of literature).

Because I want students to discard their preconceptions that classics are not to be read for pleasure but are to be crammed into a literature curriculum, and that classics can be understood only when knowledge is transferred from the teacher to the students, I end the unit on *Mill* with the conclusion of Book 1. Some students never finish the novel, but many do, having become so engaged with the Tullivers that they, like nineteenth-century readers, feel compelled to follow the family's fortunes to the end. More important, no student completes the unit with an aversion to the *Mill* or with a conviction that this novel is intended only for highbrow readers.

Admittedly, this approach neglects the finished product as an example of the way a great author successfully amalgamates the many elements of fiction into a unified whole. But by using journal writing to discover meaning and by concentrating on reading assignments of a manageable length, students improve their analytic abilities and become familiar with a reasoning process that they can apply in any academic discipline. They also enjoy the assignment.

3 Units for Specific Titles: Grades K-8

Stirring Up Shakespeare in the Elementary School

Carole Cox
Louisiana State University, Baton Rouge

While I firmly believe that children in grades 3 through 6 should have the chance to produce and perform certain of Shakespeare's plays edited especially for them,[1] another approach to his classic stories is the playing of selected scenes. This allows for the participation of children in grades K through 12, and may also become a unified school effort to share the timeless plays of the world's greatest storyteller with children.

I recently tried these last two approaches during an annual "I Love Reading Week" program called "Stirring Up Shakespeare." Instead of asking the usual guest author to speak, the principal at Walnut Hills Elementary School had invited me to introduce all the children in the school to the plays of William Shakespeare and the life and times of Renaissance England. While I have been producing Shakespeare's plays with children in the classroom and during summer programs for many years, I had never taken on an entire school, with students from a wide variety of backgrounds, at one time, nor had I focused on scenes only.

The librarian and teachers had prepared for the week by turning the library into a center for the study of Shakespeare and the Renaissance, using the sources listed in the bibliography. I further prepared the teachers and children with a brief talk about Shakespeare, and showed the entire school slides and films of the plays I have produced with children during a "Shakespeare for Kids" program I direct in Baton Rouge each summer.

I also prepared three scripts adapted from both the witches' scenes in *Macbeth* (act 1, scene 1 and act 4, scene 1) for each of three grade levels for the children and teachers to read and discuss before we were to play the scenes together.

Adapting Scenes from Shakespeare

In order to adapt scenes or an entire play from Shakespeare, I work in a paperback copy and underline what I think is most important and

manageable for the age of child who will use the script. This is primarily
a process of deleting what I think will take the play beyond the reach of
the children: scenes and characters peripheral to the main plot, lines not
critical to the further development of the main plot, and long soliloquies.
Don't underestimate children, however. I am constantly amazed at their
capacity to comprehend and act on Shakespeare's words. And I have
never changed his words, never thought I should, and never found this to
be a problem for children acting out his plays.

Here is an example of the three scripts for the two witches' scenes
from *Macbeth* adapted for three age levels: two versions of act 4, scene 1
for grades K-1 and 2-3 and act 1, scenes 1 and 3 for grades 4 and above.

A Witches' Scene from *Macbeth* (Act 4, Scene 1)
Adapted for Grades K-1

Scene—A cavern. In the middle, a boiling cauldron. Thunder. Enter the
three witches.

> *First Witch:* Round about the cauldron go.
>   *All:* Double, double, toil and trouble;
>   Fire burn and cauldron bubble.
> *Second Witch:* Fillet of a fenny snake,
>   In the cauldron boil and bake.
>   *All:* Double, double, toil and trouble;
>   Fire burn and cauldron bubble.
> *Third Witch:* Scale of dragon, tooth of wolf,
>   Witches' mummy, maw of shark.
>   *All:* Double, double, toil and trouble;
>   Fire burn and cauldron bubble.

Grades 2-3

Scene—A cavern. In the middle, a boiling cauldron. Thunder. Enter the
three witches.

> *First Witch:* Round about the cauldron go:
>   In the poison'd entrails throw.
>   *All:* Double, double, toil and trouble;
>   Fire burn and cauldron bubble.
> *Second Witch:* Fillet of a fenny snake,
>   In the cauldron boil and bake.
>   Eye of newt and toe of frog,
>   Wool of bat and tongue of dog.
>   *All:* Double, double, toil and trouble;
>   Fire burn and cauldron bubble.

> *Third Witch:* Scale of dragon, tooth of wolf,
> Witches' mummy, maw of the salt-sea shark,
> Root of hemlock digged i' the dark.
> *All:* Double, double, toil and trouble;
> Fire burn and cauldron bubble.
> *First Witch:* Cool it with a baboon's blood.
> *Second Witch:* Then the charm is firm and good.
> *Third Witch:* By the pricking of my thumbs,
> Something wicked this way comes:
> Open, locks,
> Whoever knocks!

A Witches' Scene from *Macbeth* (Act 1, Scenes 1 and 3)
Adapted for Grades 4 and Above

Scene—Scotland. A deserted place. Thunder and lightning. Enter three witches.

> *First Witch:* When shall we three meet again
> In thunder, lightning, or in rain?
> *Second Witch:* When the hurlyburly's done,
> When the battle's lost and won.
> *Third Witch:* That will be ere the set of sun.
> *First Witch:* Where the place?
> *Second Witch:* Upon the heath.
> *Third Witch:* There to meet with Macbeth.
> *All:* Fair is foul, and foul is fair.
> Hover though the fog and filthy air.

(Drum within.)

> *Third Witch:* A drum, a drum!
> Macbeth doth come.
> *All:* The weird sisters, hand in hand
> Posters of the sea and land,
> Thus do go about, about:
> Thrice to thine, and thrice to mine,
> And thrice again, to make up nine.
> Peace! the charm's wound up.

(Enter Macbeth and Banquo.)

> *Macbeth:* So foul and fair a day I have not seen.
> *Banquo:* What are these
> So wither'd, and so wild in their attire?
> *Macbeth:* Speak, if you can: what are you?

   First Witch: All hail, Macbeth! hail to thee, thane of Glamis!
 Second Witch: All hail, Macbeth! hail to thee, thane of Cawdor!
  Third Witch: All hail, Macbeth, that shalt be King hereafter!
   First Witch: Hail!
 Second Witch: Hail!
  Third Witch: Hail!
   First Witch: Lesser than Macbeth, and greater.
 Second Witch: Not so happy, yet much happier.
  Third Witch: Thou shalt get kings, though thou be none:
         So all hail, Macbeth and Banquo!
   First Witch: Banquo and Macbeth, all hail!
    Macbeth: Stay, you imperfect speakers, tell me more:
         I know I am thane of Glamis;
         But how of Cawdor? The thane of Cawdor lives,
         A prosperous gentleman; and to be king
         Stands not within the prospect of belief,
         No more than to be Cawdor. Say from whence
         You owe this strange intelligence?
         Speak, I charge you.   *(Witches vanish.)*

Playing Scenes from Shakespeare

Teachers in the school received copies of one of the three scenes adapted for their grade level. They read and discussed them with their classes. Then the gym was turned into a witches' cavern on a deserted heath in Scotland, complete with murals and art created by the children, a large black pot, and assorted rags, capes, hoods, brooms, and child-made ingredients for the witches' brew: "eye of newt and toe of frog," etc.

 As each class came to the gym, the teacher and I moved them through each scene. With younger children, three witches took turns saying their lines as the rest of the class sat in a circle and chanted the refrain for *All:* "Double, double, toil and trouble; Fire burn and cauldron bubble." Here is a step-by-step approach to playing the adapted witches' scene with an entire class in grades K through 3.

 1. Divide the whole class into three groups and seat them in a semi-circle around a cauldron (a large pot, or what have you).

 2. Speak lines to all children as they repeat them softly.

 3. Have the students practice chanting lines softly and with expression until they are fairly comfortable with them. Enthusiasm and energy are

important here rather than exactness or enunciation. The lines can be divided as follows:

First Witch:	Group 1
All:	Entire class
Second Witch:	Group 2
All:	Entire class
Third Witch:	Group 3

4. Ask for a volunteer from each group to come forward to be a witch around the cauldron. Repeat the lines in step 3 again with all the children —the standing witches and the seated class.

5. When children appear confident, let the standing witches say their lines alone while seated children chant the refrain along with the standing witches.

6. When this succeeds, dim the lights and add motions, gestures, and sound effects, as well as special effects like dry ice for the pot.

7. Repeat the above procedure over several periods, adding gestures, costume pieces, props, sound effects, and so on, until every child who wants to be a witch has had the opportunity.

Fourth- through sixth-grade children can play the characters of Macbeth and Banquo as well as the scene with the witches. One group of three boys at Walnut Hills practiced the witches' scene at home and came to school in costumes, ready to present it the day we worked with the whole class. When children are not playing a speaking part, encourage them to support the players with sound effects and the sound of the drum.

By the time the week was over, every child in the school had stepped into the role of a witch, Macbeth, or Banquo, and served as a member of the chorus, crew, and audience.

Classroom Activities Related to Classic Scenes from Shakespeare

Lynn Lastrapes, a second-grade teacher at Walnut Hills, describes what took place in her classroom as a result of "Stirring Up Shakespeare" in the entire school:

> I truthfully wondered how second graders could understand some of the complicated plots and characterizations. Except for your talk to us, I never would have thought to try this myself. I didn't take to Shakespeare until after college and I was an English major! I felt excited, stimulated, and good the whole week. I still do. I loved it for myself, but even more for the way my class took to it. Even poor students loved it. They all seemed to relish the "meatiness" of the

stories. There was so much going on. Their interest was thrilling. Since we started Shakespeare, many things have happened in our classroom.

—We read fifteen to twenty minutes of Shakespeare after lunch every day and have completed four plays. They are able to remember and compare things in all.

—Vocabulary is greatly enhanced with little effort from me.

—Predicting what was going to happen in plays was fun and meaningful.

—Recapping events at various points as we resumed our reading each day was necessary to understanding that day's part of the play and was highly accurate.

—Children could tell the play in their own words.

—We drew pictures of the plays.

—We found places in Shakespeare's plays on the map.

—We imagined the feelings of his characters and shared how we would feel if we were so-and-so.

—We listened to music like Mendelssohn's "A Midsummer Night's Dream" and Pavarotti singing the aria "O figli miei! Ah! la paterna mano" in which Macduff is thinking of how Macbeth murdered his children. (They were moved, I tell you! Even though it was in Italian, they felt the emotion.)

—We listened to Tchaikovsky's "Fantasy Overture to Romeo and Juliet." (The love theme made one of my boys do a nosedive, but he really loved it inside I think!)

—We used *Romeo and Juliet* as one of our stories during Brotherhood Week and talked about the consequences of not being brotherly to others.

—Several of my students just called and thanked me for letting them know about an LSU production of *Hamlet*. They went and loved it. Second graders going to *Hamlet* is beautiful!

—Children are clamoring for more Shakespeare.

—I want to do *The Tempest* next year. I want more too.

Teachers in other classrooms described other activities that ensued:

—Doing research and writing on Shakespeare's life and related Renaissance topics: food, arms and weapons, music, costumes and clothing, etc.

—Playing other scenes from other plays: Mark Antony's funeral oration in *Julius Caesar* and scenes from *Romeo and Juliet*.

—Listening to recordings of Shakespeare's plays.

—Reading related books about Shakespeare, his plays, and the Renaissance.

A Schoolwide Renaissance Fair

A Renaissance Fair was held one evening in conjunction with a Book Fair after two weeks of concentrated school and classroom activities designed for "Stirring Up Shakespeare." The gym was decorated with the art and writings of the children. Teachers, children, and their parents came in Renaissance dress. Renaissance theater treats of mead and gingersnaps were served. A Renaissance recorder group from LSU played during the Book Fair and then several classes presented what they had done for the whole group of teachers, children, parents, and visitors: the witches' scenes played by the kindergarten, first, and second grades, the funeral oration scene from *Julius Caesar* played by third-graders, scenes from *Romeo and Juliet* played by fifth-graders, a report on Renaissance music and a performance on recorders by fifth-graders, and a report, display, and demonstration of Renaissance arms and weaponry by fourth-graders.

The event later was the lead article in the award-winning school newspaper *Paw Prints:*

Learning About the Renaissance

I love the exciting times of the Renaissance! I hope you like to get in touch with the Renaissance world like I do.

Dr. Carole Cox Spates, a teacher from LSU, came to Walnut Hills. She showed us books, costumes, and great scenes by William Shakespeare, like "Hamlet," which was acted out by students.

Then her husband, Mr. Spates, taught us how to use a sword, and how the people used the sword in the Renaissance times. It was a lot of entertainment for me! But, the guy who was fencing against me won the fight.

Thursday, February 16, I came with my parents to a Renaissance party at school. It was very exciting for me too, because I was wearing a Renaissance costume.

It's true that I didn't act in a scene. But I was a stage manager. Next year I will be sure to participate in a scene from Shakespeare at school.

A 5th-Grader

Articles by many children filled the pages. Two of the children's comments underscore the impact of this new approach to the classics: a schoolwide exploration of the life, times, and works of William Shakespeare.

Shakespeare was a magnificent man. He was a play writer. He wrote plays such as *Macbeth, Hamlet, Julius Caesar,* and *Romeo and Juliet.* Feb. 16 we relived his plays. It was as if Shakespeare were inside us. Shakespeare will always live because of his plays.

A 5th-Grader

All around the school of Walnut Hills, kids and teachers have been talking about Shakespeare. Everyone knows he's a wonderful person, and he's been writing stories like *Macbeth, Hamlet,* and more. Even now he's gone, we still are looking back to his stories and enjoying them.

A 3rd-Grader

Notes

1. Carole Cox, "Shakespeare & Co.: The Best in Classroom Reading and Drama," *The Reading Teacher* 33 (Jan. 1980): 438-41.

References

Brooks, Polly Schoyer, and Nancy Zinsser Walworth. *The World Awakes: The Renaissance in Western Europe.* New York: Lippincott, 1962.

Brown, John Russell. *Shakespeare and His Theatre.* New York: Lothrop, Lee & Shepard, 1982.

Chute, Marchette. *Stories from Shakespeare.* New York: New American Library, 1976.

Gorsline, Douglas. *What People Wore.* New York: Bonanza Books, 1953.

Green, Roger Lancelyn. *Tales from Shakespeare,* 2 vols. London: Gollancz, 1964–65.

Hodges, C. Walter. *Shakespeare's Theatre.* New York: Coward-McCann, 1966.

Horizon Magazine Editors. *Shakespeare's England.* New York: American Heritage, 1964.

Kirtland, G. B. *One Day in Elizabethan England.* New York: Harcourt Brace Jovanovich, 1962.

Lamb, Charles, and Mary Lamb. *Tales from Shakespeare.* New York: Dutton, 1979.

Reese, M. M. *William Shakespeare.* London: Edward Arnold, 1963.

Shakespeare, William. Pendulum illustrated series of twelve plays with student activity books by Linda A. Cadrain. West Haven, Conn.: Pendulum Press, 1980.

Shakespeare, William. *Seeds of Time,* selections compiled by Bernice Grohskopf. New York: Atheneum, 1963.

Updike, John, ed. *Bottom's Dream: Adapted from William Shakespeare's A Midsummer Night's Dream,* with music by Felix Mendelssohn. New York: Alfred A. Knopf, 1969.

White, Anne Terry. *Will Shakespeare and the Globe Theater.* New York: Random House, 1955.

Using an Aesop Fable for a Lesson in Values

Samuel A. Perez
University of Oregon, Eugene

Walter C. Parker
University of Texas, Arlington

Fables are a requisite component of any child's knowledge of the classics of children's literature. And, as children's literature, they can be used to transmit our cultural heritage, help children understand other people, help children better understand themselves, expose children to excellent writing, stimulate an enjoyment of reading, and teach children concepts about literature.[1] One such concept students can learn from fables is an understanding of values.

Values are the belief system one holds about what is important. We study values with students through a process called values clarification, which is an attempt to help students analyze the values they hold, both the ones they can verbalize and the ones that underlie their actual behavior. Through the reading and discussion of fables, students can explore their beliefs and the consequences of acting on those beliefs. The goal of values lessons is to have students choose from among values, choose consistently and knowingly, and develop and act upon their own value systems.[2]

Aesop's fables are probably the best known of all fables. They have become true classics of children's literature because they have wisdom, charm, and universal truths that are just as relevant today as they were centuries ago. The fables of Aesop also lend themselves to discussion and to activities through which students can examine their own values. They are ideal for values lessons for several reasons. Their simple, clear examples of right and wrong and their animal characters appeal to students, especially young children. Aesop's fables also require little intellectual effort to generalize from the animal characters to their human counterparts, probably because of their simple plots, which usually contain only one incident or event. Still another reason is that Aesop's fables are short enough to make them easy reading for students, and long enough to make them especially suitable for discussion. And, finally, Aesop's fables are ideal for values lessons because the values in them tend to be essential, fundamental values common to all humanity. This chapter will describe a values lesson based on Aesop's fable "The Fox and the Crow." The lesson is designed for use with elementary- or middle-school students.

The first step in the lesson calls for the teacher to establish a background for reading the fable. The teacher tells students that "The Fox and the Crow" is an old fable told many years ago by the Greek slave Aesop. Students should then be told that a fable is a short, simple story that illustrates a moral lesson, and often uses animals as characters. Next, the teacher provides a background for the specific fable "The Fox and the Crow." An excellent way to do this is to direct student attention to the pictures accompanying the fable. As students view the pictures, they are asked to hypothesize the story development: What is happening? Who are the characters? Where is the story taking place? What is the message?

After interpreting the story through pictures, the teacher should check to see if students understand the vocabulary basic to the meaning of the fable. If key words need to be taught, they should be written on the chalkboard and pointed out in the context of the story. The words should then be pronounced either by the students or the teacher if needed. The meaning of the words with their written form and their use in context should be emphasized so that students will accurately and quickly fit meaning to the proper context when they encounter the words in the fable.

After the students have learned the important vocabulary, questions to guide their reading are generated, preferably by the students themselves. The questions raised during the interpretation of the pictures accompanying the fable would make excellent purpose-setting questions to give focus to student reading. The teacher should either write the purpose-setting questions on the chalkboard or have students write them in their notebooks for reference. Now, students are ready to read "The Fox and the Crow" silently, carefully noting detail to determine if their interpretation of the pictures was accurate and whether they can answer the purpose-setting questions.

After students have read the fable, a discussion is conducted around the fable's moral. The moral concluding "The Fox and the Crow" is as follows:

> The flatterer doth rob by stealth,
> His victim, both of wit and wealth.[3]

The discussion begins by eliciting from students their understanding of the fable's theme of flattery. The following values questions are suggested to guide the discussion. The second through eighth questions elicit value statements from students around the issue of flattery, and the last question encourages students to take a stand.

1. What is flattery?

2. Who would you rather have for your friend—the fox or the crow? Why?

3. When we flatter someone, do we always want something? Why or why not?

4. What do people want when they flatter others?

5. Does Aesop think it is fair or unfair to flatter someone? Why or why not?

6. When, if ever, would it be worth it to you to flatter someone?

7. What good is flattery to the flatterer?

8. Do you think flattery harms the flatterer? Why or why not?

9. What stand are you willing to take about flattery?

In using Aesop's fable "The Fox and the Crow" for a values lesson, the following guidelines must be kept in mind. First, the teacher should exhibit good questioning techniques by striving for participation of all students, waiting an adequate amount of time for students to give their responses, and asking primarily open-ended questions that elicit more than a "yes" or "no." Second, the teacher should show respect for diversity and privacy. Values discussions are not debates, and there are no right or wrong answers. The teacher should model respect and a nonjudgmental attitude, rather than agreement or disagreement, with all values expressed. Privacy must also be respected, and students who prefer not to respond should be encouraged to say simply, "I pass." Third, values lessons are for clarification, not indoctrination. The aim of a values discussion is for students to bring to their own awareness what they already believe to be good and bad, right and wrong, and to examine these values. The teacher should be careful not to persuade students to believe as he or she does, but to help students clarify what they believe.

Notes

1. See Iris M. Tiedt, "Planning an Elementary School Literature Program," *Elementary English* 47 (Feb. 1970): 193-98.

2. See Louis E. Raths, M. Harmin, and Sidney B. Simon, *Values and Teaching* (Columbus, Ohio: Charles E. Merrill, 1966).

3. In *The Fables of Aesop,* ed. Joseph Jacobs (London: Macmillan, 1894).

A Fairy Tale Revealed: *Animal Farm*

Kevin O'Neill
Tamanend Junior High School, Warrington, Pennsylvania

Animal Farm, by George Orwell, is a fairy tale filled with symbolism. As a story of talking pigs and barnyard antics, it has little problem in communicating themes of exploitation, rebellion, and hypocrisy; however, the book's concern with economic systems and historical rebellion is beyond the experience of most seventh-graders. Yet capitalism, socialism, the Russian Revolution, and totalitarianism are all integral parts of the novel and need to be included.

Before beginning this novel, it is essential for students to understand symbolism. A straightforward exercise asking students for examples of words, objects, and signs that stand for or symbolize something else solves this problem. The color blue is sky, the Statue of Liberty is freedom, and a little man on a placard is the men's room. The answers vary but the result is the same. Students are aware of what symbols are and how they are used.

By using such familiar examples as Darth Vader's representing evil and Luke Skywalker good, or our assumption that the cowboy in the white hat is the good guy and the man in black the villain, the teacher can show students that characters in stories and novels may also be used as symbols. The characters in *Animal Farm* may be talking animals in a fairy tale, but they also represent something much more.

Once the concept of symbolism has been introduced, students read chapter 1. Instead of establishing the story line—who, what, where, when, and why—a parallel exercise forces the students to apply the situation of the animals to people. Students note similarities and differences, realizing how the world of the animals has meaning on a symbolic level for humanity.

> *Parallel Exercise:* The owner of a factory pays his employees the bare minimum so he can gain the maximum amount of profit. The workers perform all of the labor, face all of the dangers at the job, and receive little in return. With the money they are paid, the

workers have just enough to pay for food, shelter, and clothing with very little left over. Out of fifty-two weeks in a year, seven days are spent on vacation and the rest are spent working. After a lifetime of service, the employees are given a gold watch and retire on Social Security, getting just enough money to survive.

Questions: Is this system fair? What would be a better way of doing things? Write a paragraph like the one above, from the animals' point of view (see Old Major's speech).

When first presented with this model, students are sympathetic to the cause of the animals and workers and thereby arrive at the same answer for solving the injustice—rebellion. Like the animals, the students argue for changing the system. Both animals on the farm and laborers in the factory should share equally in work and profit. A vocabulary should be introduced here to facilitate discussion:

Capitalism: an economic system that allows an individual to become rich through the hard work of others (practiced by Farmer Jones and the owner of the factory).

Socialism: an economic system in which individuals share equally in work and profits (the goal of the animals, the answer to employer exploitation).

Bourgeois: people who own property in society, owners (Farmer Jones and the factory owner).

Proletariat: people who work in a society, workers (the animals and the factory workers).

After establishing Farmer Jones as a capitalist bourgeois, and the animals as proletarian workers, socialism becomes a viable alternative to the seeming exploitation of animals and workers. In reading chapter 2, students identify the single most important principle of animalism as equality; however, it is also noted that the pigs become leaders and that by the end of the chapter milk is mysteriously missing and not being doled out equally.

As the novel continues, students become more aware of the problems in applying the principles of animalism/socialism. In theory, animalism/socialism is ideal; however, in application its principles can become violated and warped. To further illustrate the idealism of this system, apply it to the classroom. In the following parallel exercise students are encouraged to debate the question and decide whether the system would work in their lives.

Parallel Exercise: Let's change the system of the classroom. We will do away with a competitive grading system. Everyone will work according to his or her own capacity. Homework will not be assigned.

Students will work for themselves, not for the reward of a grade. We will share equally in work and rewards. All students will receive "Bs." Students will decide what is to be studied. There will be no teacher giving directions or orders.

After developing a personal viewpoint and reading chapter 5, students are now ready to assimilate historical details with the symbolism of the story. An informational sheet is provided which gives a brief synopsis of the Russian Revolution. Students are then asked to find characters in the book that symbolize people and events from history.

Informational Sheet: In the mid-1800s, there was a philosopher named Karl Marx. At that time, Marx looked at the major nations of the world. He said their economies were based on capitalism; individuals invested capital, money, so they could make a profit.

The trouble with capitalism, Marx said, is that some people become rich through the expense and hard work of others. Marx thought that there should be a fairer way or system to distribute the wealth of a country, so all the people could share in the profits. According to Marx, everyone should be equal. There should be no rich or poor in a country, but everyone should share equally.

Marx believed that eventually the rich in a country, the bourgeoisie, would be overthrown by the poor, the proletariat. Marx predicted that all capitalistic countries would be overthrown by their workers, who would rebel against the rich.

The writings of Marx impressed another economic philosopher and politician; his name was Lenin and he lived in Russia. Lenin adopted the writings of Marx and added some ideas of his own. Lenin believed in socialism, that the government should own and manage the production and distribution of goods for the benefit of society.

Lenin organized the workers and peasants of Russia. With the help of Trotsky, his general, the government of Russia was overthrown. Trotsky led the fighting and was recognized as a national hero. Lenin came to power and worked to establish Russia as the United Soviet Socialist Republic. Lenin worked toward the goal of socialism.

After Lenin's death two of his followers struggled for control of Russia. Trotsky and Stalin fought for political power and control. Stalin won. Trotsky was labeled by Stalin a traitor and forced to leave the country. Trotsky escaped to Mexico but was assassinated there.

Under the leadership of Stalin, the Soviet Union became a totalitarian state. The state had total control over the lives of its people, as it does today. What started out as a dream of socialism for the workers of Russia became a nightmare of totalitarianism.

Through this series of exercises that parallel the theme and spirit of *Animal Farm,* students are able to recognize symbolic meanings in the novel. At the outset socialism is filled with promise and seems an attractive alternative to capitalism. By identifying with the animals and applying the principles of their system to the classroom, students acknowledge the inherent problems of socialism and witness an idealism that does not survive the reality of human nature as we know it. Through these exercises the evils of capitalism may be exaggerated and the system of socialism simplified, but these students discovered some profound insights experienced in a direct and personal way, and were exposed to the essence of Orwell's complicated fairy tale.

Exploring Emotion through *Romeo and Juliet*

Jim Christ
Sahuarita Junior High School, Sahuarita, Arizona

"The trouble with teaching the classics is that the classics just aren't relevant" . . . "The trouble with teaching the classics is that the kids just don't appreciate what they're reading." I would wager that a language arts teacher somewhere makes a comment like one of these every day. Some of us may believe that reading and literature should only be an enjoyable and independent enterprise and do not teach works like *Julius Caesar* or *Silas Marner*. On the other hand, some of us hold that the classics are valuable for study regardless of students' subjective reactions and force-feed them *Romeo and Juliet* or *The Red Badge of Courage,* using quizzes in an effort to ensure their reading. But if a novel or a play is not relevant reading for today's students, how can it be called a classic? And, conversely, if a work were not enjoyable reading for a substantial public, how did it come to be called a classic in the first place? The real trouble with teaching the classics is that each is unique, and its uniqueness defies formulas.

It is obvious that teaching our students the classics is not an easy task, but isn't there at least a general approach to be used with most literature? I believe there is, and the strategy owes more to research in composition than it does to research in reading. I'm embarrassed to say that I nick-named it "listerature," because it involves many listing and brainstorming activities.

The first thing for the teacher to think through is what it is that the students will discover from the literature. This determination is naturally based first on the needs of the students and second on the content and structure of the piece to be studied. With eleventh-grade, college-bound students, a teacher may want to develop the uses of dialect in the *Adventures of Huckleberry Finn*. With average ninth-graders, a teacher may use that same novel to work toward an understanding of what friendship means.

Once the teacher determines which work is appropriate and which of its aspects will be emphasized, the unit proceeds with reading and with class discussions that are very much like the prewriting activity of brainstorming. The concluding activity is usually a composition assignment with ample encouragement to revise and edit the written piece until it is finished and polished.

Last year when selecting a work for my eighth-graders to read near the end of the school year, I almost did not choose *Romeo and Juliet*. One of my students was in a state of severe depression, and I thought that the suicides of Romeo and Juliet might be worse than inappropriate. I finally did choose the play because its portrayal of teenage love is indeed so relevant to eighth-graders and because, after all, one of the things Shakespeare is telling us in this tragedy is that reason must govern and temper our emotions. My first task was complete then—I had matched masterpiece to class and decided to focus on one important theme. This is perhaps the most important phase of developing the unit. Once the teacher is sure that the students can respond to the selected theme, what remains is to focus attention on it. The remainder of the "listerature" strategy is presented in six steps.

1. Before reading a single word of the work, introduce the selection with a brainstorming session that is both a prewriting-listing activity (as if we were about to write a composition) and a preface to the theme about to be studied. It is necessary to formulate questions on the basis of the work's theme that will help students discover what they already know.

Romeo and Juliet may be introduced with questions such as "What makes people fight?" and "What makes people fall in love?" Notice that these initial questions are much more concrete than the theme of "reason governing emotion," yet the relationship is clear. Notice also that these are good discovery questions for eighth-graders, who have already formed some notions about reasons for fighting and falling in love.

Eighth graders will probably give these reasons for fighting: "getting mad," "helping a friend who's in a fight," "getting even for something," "protecting someone else," and "defending yourself," among others. For falling in love they will often list: "emotions" (I found many eighth-graders who felt that love was an emotion over which people had no control), "good looks," and "being sexy." I got many responses dealing with the sexual qualities of love—I encouraged these despite some giggles because children know that sexuality and love are related and also because Romeo and Juliet have such a strong physical attraction.

It is wise to end the session with other questions that will lead into the work being studied. With *Romeo and Juliet,* these might be: "Are there times when it's best not to fight, even when we are angry?" and "Do people ever *decide* whom they are going to love or how much they are going to fall in love?" Students should keep a copy of their notes from the brainstorming session to refer to as the reading progresses.

2. Read and discuss the work. Some readings should be done in class so that teachers can identify those students who might need more individual help or further motivation. The teacher should read the same book at the same time during class, as a modeling procedure. With drama much (if not all) of the reading ought to be performed aloud in class. With reading that might be difficult for some students, such as *Romeo and Juliet,* the teacher ought to assign parts the day before and have students practice reading through sections. I believe that the teacher should also read a part each day, expressing enjoyment of the reading and adding appropriate inflections. Students are much more likely to perform a dramatic reading—an oral interpretation—if they see and hear their teacher reading with vigor and emotion.

Discussion must not only answer questions that the student has, but also should center on previous discovery questions and brainstorming. Students will see fights occurring for all the reasons they had suggested: Tybalt gets angry, most of the Montagues and Capulets come running to help a friend in the opening scene, Romeo must get even for the death of Mercutio, and so on. Point out to students that neither side reasons; there is no effort to control anger. With the love at first sight between Romeo and Juliet, it is again obvious that neither attempts to use reason. Romeo and Juliet are drawn together by one another's physical attractiveness, by sexuality, and generally by their emotions. Their love is real, but students can now be asked to start considering whether it is wise to simply obey our *feelings* of love and hate.

3. One or more prewriting-listing activities should be employed in the midst of the reading. The brainstorming or discussion questions here must serve two purposes: to ensure that the student is reading and understanding the selection and to examine further the theme. After students have read through the fight scenes involving Mercutio, Tybalt, and Romeo, they begin to see that many things are going wrong for the protagonists. At this time it is appropriate to ask, "How do Romeo and Juliet attempt to solve their problems?" and "Are these actions reasonable?" and "What else might they have tried?" Students will identify the influence of chance or fate in the destruction of Romeo and Juliet, but they will also notice that Romeo and Juliet continue to obey only their emotions. Students will even ask why Romeo and Juliet do not simply announce their marriage after its consummation. (Notice that the purpose here is not to study the structure of tragedy or Elizabethan drama. It is simply to read a masterpiece and to think about it.) As they did with the first listing activity, students should save their lists for reference.

4. Continue reading and discussing the ways in which the story is answering our questions.

5. After the reading is complete, initiate composing processes through a final prewriting-listing activity. This might be done in brainstorm fashion, or independently, to encourage more variation in the essays. The main goal for students to achieve is a fairly crystallized opinion regarding the theme of the work.

When I most recently taught *Romeo and Juliet,* I asked my students to prepare a list of answers to the question "Who were all the people that helped cause Romeo's and Juliet's deaths?" As they listed each character, they were to make a remark or two on how this character acted reasonably or emotionally in the play. I helped them with these lists, although very few students needed or requested help. Finally, I asked students to write an analysis of who was most responsible for the destruction of Romeo and Juliet. I asked students to consider emotion and reasonable behavior as they wrote. Most students laid the heaviest blame upon Romeo and Juliet themselves, though their parents did not escape indictment. No matter who was blamed in the tragedy, nearly all students—even the youngster who had been so depressed—expressed the opinion that unreasoned obedience to feelings and emotions is unsound.

6. The final and optional step is to extend the unit. The teacher must decide if this examination of theme has gone far enough, and evaluate where the discussion has taken the class after reading *Romeo and Juliet.* If the students were especially interested in the nature of love, it might be profitable to read a short story such as O. Henry's "Gift of the Magi" or a novel like Norma Klein's *Queen of the What Ifs* (New York: Fawcett, 1982). Students might want to do more thinking about obedience to parents, and then *Huckleberry Finn* might be a good choice.

I apologize for calling my method "listerature," but listing techniques have seemed especially useful to me in my classroom because I have always believed strongly in a composition-centered language arts classroom.

4 Units for Specific Titles: High School

Cracking an Old Chestnut: "Ozymandias"

Joyce Kinkead
Utah State University, Logan

The class clown usually greets my introduction to "Ozymandias" with a Joan Rivers, finger-in-the-mouth, "Percy *Bysshe* Shelley—what a wimp." However, by providing what Louise Rosenblatt describes as "fruitful interactions"[1] between the high-school student and the literary work, we can actually help even the class clown come away from "Ozymandias" with a new perspective on "that Percy guy." Using probing questions, creative dramatics, and purposeful writing tasks, we can help students crack an old "chestnut."

Probing questions should do just that: probe the student's mind for an interpretation of the literary work to help the student visualize the poem. After hearing the poem, the students read the text, then focus on class discussion prompted by the following questions:

1. What kind of feeling do you have after reading this poem? Why?
2. What happens in the poem?
3. Who is "I"?
4. Who is the traveler and what does he or she look like?
5. Where does this meeting take place? (There is no textual evidence for an answer to this question; it is purely in the varied imaginations of the students.)
6. When does this meeting occur?
7. How did the "I" and the "traveler" get together?
8. What is an "antique land"? Where do you imagine this poem to be set?
9. Describe the statue. Who was Ozymandias?
10. What kind of personality was Ozymandias? What kind of ruler? How do you know these things? (Give examples from the poem to support your beliefs.)

73

11. Let's look at the fourth character in our drama: what was the sculptor like? What did he think of Ozymandias? (Support your answer.) Why did he design the statue?

12. Why did Ozymandias pick out that motto? What does it say about him?

13. What is ironic in this poem?

14. What does survive the years?

15. What would you say is the theme of this poem?

16. What is this poem saying about art and power?

17. Identify alliteration, symbols, images.

18. Why did Ozymandias want this statue built?

Certainly some of these questions call for conjecture on the part of the students, but that conjecture helps them to gain an image of the poem, its characters, its time, and its theme. That image can be enhanced by creative dramatics, using "minimal situations" as James Moffett and Betty Jane Wagner suggest.[2] The first dramatic exercise might simply be a warm-up: what does a sneer of cold command look like? A more complex exercise would involve pairing off the students for an audience between king and artist. The sculptor has been called to the ruler to receive instructions on building a statue in Ozymandias' honor. How would each act and react? How does the sculptor "mock" the king and still keep his head? This dialogue would require only a few minutes. To involve the entire group, it is possible to do a crowd scene. For example, what is it like after a hard day's work for the laborers as they sit around the communal soup pot in the evening? Is there any unrest among the group? How would each laborer react to an agitator? This five-minute drama gives the students a feel for the times and for the mass of people not mentioned in the poem but certainly involved.

Writing assignments continue to build the feeling for the poem stimulated by these interactions. Too often, we see the critical essay as the sole mode of discourse. Certainly, it is valuable to explore the importance of art in society, but many students will respond better to writing assignments that involve them further in the poem. Using the laborers once again, students could as these characters write letters to distant relatives explaining their situation. Or the sculptor might write home to his family, expressing his distaste for the king but enjoying the opportunity for patron-supported artistic work. Perhaps the king has ordered a proclamation at the unveiling of his statue. What does the communique between Ozymandias' enemies say? Write Ozymandias' obituary. Be a historian and report the end of Ozymandias' reign. What was the traveler's journal entry upon viewing the ruins of the king's statue?

The questions and activities for "Ozymandias" are limited only by the teacher's imagination. It is up to us to stretch our own imaginations so that our students are not limited to barren readings of literature and one-sided lectures. Then our class clown might well ask, "What else did this guy write?"

Notes

1. Louise Rosenblatt, *Literature as Exploration,* 3d rev. ed. (New York: Noble & Noble, 1968), 26.

2. James Moffett and Betty Jane Wagner, *Student-Centered Language Arts and Reading, K-13: A Handbook for Teachers,* 2d ed. (Boston: Houghton Mifflin, 1976), 96.

Dickens and Company, "Recalled to Life"

Karen Kays
Sherman High School, Sherman, Texas

When I was moved from middle school to the high school, I was excited about the fact that I would get to teach more literature, but I groaned when I was told our major novel for freshman English was *Great Expectations* by Charles Dickens. I had not read much Dickens, but what I had read I did not like. The students groaned just as I had, because they had heard about *Great Expectations* from older students. The first year, I gave the typical lecture on the life and works of Charles Dickens, we read and discussed the novel, and we did character sketches and other writing activities. I did not feel good about the unit when we finished and knew that I had to do something to make Dickens and *Great Expectations* more interesting. How could I get the students to want to read this novel and other novels by Dickens?

First, I had to become more interested myself and the way to do that was to become more knowledgeable, so I began reading books and articles about Dickens. The more I read, the more interested I became. He became a real person for me, and I thought, "If only I could make the students see him that way." Then the idea hit me. I would become Charles Dickens for a day. I rented a costume—a suit straight out of the Victorian period, a cravat, a top hat, and a walking stick. I put together all the information about Dickens that I had gathered, and I incorporated lots of little tidbits that are not found in a typical biography. The day before my presentation, the students were told to be on their best behavior the next day because we were having a guest speaker from London, England. They were intrigued.

On the day of my presentation, I did not go to my classes. A fellow teacher checked attendance for me and told the students that I was absent. Then she introduced their guest speaker. Charles Dickens entered the room and told about himself—his life, his feelings, his beliefs, and his works. I, as Charles Dickens, acted the way that I believed he would have. I did not tell what he was like; I showed what he was like. The students loved it, and because they had met Mr. Dickens in person, they were much more interested in him. Some even went to the library to check out books written by Dickens, books that he had talked about. At any rate, when we began to read *Great Expectations,* they were more eager than they had been before.

After the students had begun to read the novel, I assigned oral character sketches. They were to do just what I had done with Dickens, that is, choose a character and become that person. They were responsible for the interpretation of the characters that they chose and for their costumes, so they had to do some careful reading and some research on the Victorian period. What a success this was! We had a young Pip who told about his sister and his fear of a convict. We had an older Pip who had become a gentleman. There was a cruel, conceited Estella, a Mrs. Joe waving Tickler, a convict wearing a leg iron, a blacksmith, and many others. Most of the sketches were excellent and brought the book to life for us.

Having Charles Dickens as a guest of the freshman English classes has become a tradition at our high school. Some still groan when *Great Expectations* is mentioned, but many want to know if and when Charles Dickens is coming, and many are looking ahead to see what characters they want to portray. Since many of the sophomores, juniors, and seniors have been characters from *Great Expectations,* I now use them to help introduce the novel to the freshmen. When Charles Dickens comes all the way from London to tell about himself and his works, he brings with him some of the main characters from *Great Expectations.* They do not do a complete sketch; they tell just enough about themselves to make everyone listening want to read the novel.

Once a year, Charles Dickens and *Great Expectations* come to life at our high school, and I believe that Dickens, who loved the stage and loved to perform, would heartily approve.

Make It a Mystery—And Let Your Students Be the Villains!

Margaret Dodson
Borah High School, Boise, Idaho

The modern classic short story "I'm a Fool," by Sherwood Anderson, fascinates high-school students with issues directly relevant to their lives. The story of a young man on his own in a world of fast horses, whiskey, and gambling is enticing enough, but students will also learn the agony that can accompany making one's own decisions and the pain caused by one's own errors. Walter, as he calls himself, tells a lie. Not such a bad lie, he thinks, at first, anyway . . . but problems arise.

Introduce the story by discussing with the students the times when we are all tempted to lie, even the times we do lie. Not a student in the room can resist. Everyone has told a "little" lie, even one that "solved" a problem. In fact, there is often a sense of delight in considering the cleverness with which we adroitly explain the faults of someone else, or the impossibility of completing a task. Lying can seem to be, after all, a pretty good friend and tactic.

Next, quiet the room by asking about the times when the lies did not work, the times when the lies have led to greater and greater trouble. Without dwelling too long on this aspect of the lie, read the following statement.

> We are going to read a story in which a young man, who is having a great time, tells "just a little lie"—that grows bigger and bigger. And then, more than anything else in the world, he wishes he had told the truth, because he has fallen in love with the woman he lied to. As you read the story, be thinking of what you would do if you were in the same situation. Would you have the courage to take a chance on winning by telling the truth? Or would you be too ashamed, clinging to the lie without any hope of rescuing yourself or your love?

To facilitate the "mystery," have copies of the story made, omitting the first paragraph (which makes the outcome of the story too clear) and stopping the story at this point.

> Lucy she says, "We got to go to the train now," and she was most crying too, but she never knew nothing I knew, and she couldn't be so all busted up. And then, before Wilbur and Miss Woodbury got up to where we was, she put her face up and kissed me quick and put her head up against me and she was all quivering and—Gee whizz.

After students read the story, ask the following questions.

> What will Walter do?
>
> Will he tell Lucy who he really is before she leaves?
>
> Will Lucy forgive him if he does tell her?
>
> Or will Lucy write to him in Marietta, only to have the letters returned, marked Person Unknown?
>
> Does he owe Lucy the truth?

Following the discussion, assign students to "finish the story." Older students may be assigned a thesis-argument paper. Students of all ages will enjoy writing a creative-narrative paper "ending" the story. In either case, clarify the writer's position, directing students to write either as they themselves would react, or as they hope the story will turn out. Be prepared to give students adequate time to deal with the complex set of feelings they are experiencing and the value decision to be made.

"I'm a Fool" is rich with other possibilities that can be worked into this activity. The vernacular style of the story reveals many differences normally found between speech and the written word. The time period and setting of the story develop an understanding of early twentieth-century America, including the social issues of class and color. These and other aspects of the story work well with upper-level students. If the reading level of the story is too difficult for younger students, there is an excellent film of "I'm a Fool" produced by Perspective Films (1978). Shutting the projector off at just the right moment creates the same mystery as the unfinished story.

As the final activity, have students read each other's papers. Although proofreading and peer editing time is always valuable, with this assignment you will want to encourage sharing of the final versions. When everyone is ready, read the conclusion of the original story to the students—but do not be surprised if many of them prefer their own endings to Sherwood Anderson's. "I'm a Fool" will have become a part of their lives, with a personal meaning that only a true classic can achieve.

It's a Sin to Kill *Mockingbird*

Steven Athanases
High School District 214, Arlington Heights
and Buffalo Grove, Illinois

A child of the sixties, I made my teaching mission clear: inspire young minds, inculcate values, humanize the institution of high school. But like so many of any generation, I chose English teaching specifically because I love literature and want students to love it, too. And, like so many English teachers, I have found the source of one of my greatest challenges and greatest frustrations to be that students, in general, don't care much for the stuff, much less love it. So with great care I choose literature I think is not only moving, wonderful, and *significant,* but accessible to the eighties adolescent who enters my tenth-grade literature class. And still too many come to the books unequipped and blasé and leave the books wondering what I see in them that makes them such a big deal to me.

Oh, sure, I can give them the pat statements about how this work fits into the body of American literature, how it presents a microcosm of society, pins down some eternal human truth. Or I could put the novels in nutshells as my eleventh-grade teacher did, telling them to memorize for Wednesday's test Tindall's theory of *The Return of the Native:* a Darwinian man in a Newtonian environment scrutinized by a Victorian society. And most would memorize it dutifully but be no richer for it.

But I subscribe to Louise Rosenblatt's notion that reading is transaction, that reader and text interact, and that the student's most significant reward from literature comes from that personalized interaction with a text. I hope for this, but find that even a book as seemingly accessible as Harper Lee's *To Kill a Mockingbird* needs help with my upper-middle-class, raised-on-TV-and-Atari teens. So I search for techniques to open up *Mockingbird* for these students to make it a rich experience for them.

Boo Radley: Sharing Legends

These students who face me daily are adolescent, I remind myself, struggling to mature, spouting "I'm sure!" to silliness. And much of the intrigue surrounding Boo seems silly and insignificant to many from this "mature" vantage point. To try to recapture the joy and excitement of a mysterious, frightening character, I precede the novel with a session of legend-telling in a circle, lights off, curtains drawn.

I tell in hushed tones and graphic detail the Cuba Road story we told in my hometown, about the couple who run out of gas on the secluded country road and the escaped convict who decapitates the young man and strings him up in a tree for his girlfriend to see. Half a dozen students per class know the story by some other name, with some other details, and they share, excitedly, their variations. "What other local legends do we know?" I ask. Someone tells the babysitter story, about the murderous phone caller who we learn is on the phone extension upstairs in the house where the fifteen-year-old girl is babysitting. Someone else tells about the Mad Rocker, who could be seen, until his recent death, rocking furiously in the second-story window of his home four blocks from school. And other stories are told, legends bared, many familiar tales about some other spooky character or incident, others new to the group, but all creating just the intrigue, the sense of mystery needed. And we discuss what these legends share (a mysterious character, a vulnerable victim, a close call), why we tell them, and what keeps them alive, all of which makes students eager to get their own red-hot copies of a novel that begins with the legend of a man who haunts a town.

Discrimination: Role-Playing

But now I must get these students to care about Tom Robinson and his trial, to grieve with Jem when the jury finds a black man guilty of raping a white woman he only helped. But my students in this WASPy suburb told me years ago they hadn't known much discrimination other than what they had seen in movies or heard "from a friend who told me he had a friend who . . ." Again, I need some student immersion into the theme to generate personal responses. I get some role-playing volunteers to enact three scenes of serious concern, exaggerated here for easy illustration and comic effect:

1. *Job interview* for laboratory research position—a male employer, a male applicant, two female applicants: the employer calls in prospective employees one at a time, ending with the male. The women hold advanced degrees in the physical sciences from prestigious universities, have years of laboratory research at top-notch institutions, and come with folders full of letters of reference. The male applicant passed a P.E. class at the community college, drove a delivery truck one summer, and has only a letter from his mom crumpled in his back jeans pocket. The employer,

cool to the two women, immediately talks sports to the man, slaps him on the back, and hires him.

2. *Courtroom Scene*—male judge, suburban housewife and mother, male teenage driver, and female teenage witness: The woman is obviously guilty of causing the collision in front of the grocery store, but the judge stereotypes the teenage driver ("So you're only sixteen, huh? Not a lot of experience behind the wheel. Were you distracted by the radio or anything?") and his witness ("You're not going steady with this driver, are you?") and sides with the woman who has age on her side ("I hope the little ones weren't hurt by this").

3. *Family Scene on Report Card Day*—mom, dad, teenage girl, teenage boy: one child once again earned straight As and the adulation of the parents, while the other ("What report card?"), passing only P.E. with a D, is scolded, criticized, and compared to the first. The stellar student is treated to some new clothing that night and the other is banished to dishwashing and the books.

The scenes are examined for parallels: who had the power in the scene? How was it abused? What did the losers lose? How might the power-holders have better used their power? These scenes illustrate discrimination and heighten students' awareness of this theme and its implications as they read about treatment of blacks by whites in 1930s Maycomb County, Alabama.

Close Reading: Research Groups

The eighties student, who too often cannot or will not attend to the written word, too seldom engages in close reading, a careful examination of textual and contextual clues that help a reader make meaning. Research groups can help demand close reading and full student attention and involvement. Students are broken into small groups to research the following issues, take notes on findings, and present results to the class:

1. Significance of the book title
2. Themes, lessons, messages from the book
3. Boo Radley: legend and reality
4. Evidence of discrimination against blacks
5. Atticus as father and lawyer
6. Jem's maturation
7. Scout as young girl and detached narrator
8. Key events of the trial (presented through brief enactment of the trial scene rather than as traditional report)

Follow-up: The Film and Related Literature

Indelible performances by Gregory Peck and Mary Badham as Atticus and Scout are reason enough to order a videotape of the 1962 film for a class showing and follow-up discussion. But other issues deserve attention: What are the gains and losses of this film adaptation? Do the film portrayals suit the characters etched by Harper Lee? How does the filmmaker attempt to preserve Lee's first-person narration? (Voice-over narration using Lee's actual voice, mood of music, and camera angle to dramatize the Boo Radley legend.)

Once students have dealt with the theme of racial discrimination, other fine works can reinforce the issues: Faulkner's "Dry September," which depicts a similar situation but one which results in a lynching; Tom McAfee's "This is My Living Room,"[1] the disturbing monologue of an angry bigot; and James Baldwin's *If Beale Street Could Talk,* the first-person account of a young black woman's struggle to remain strong despite terrible odds.

Harper Lee's novel remains an important one because of its sensitive examination of prejudice, innocence and experience, family relationships, issues of conscience, and perspective-taking. Activities such as those described here can help the eighties high-school student realize the rich rewards of this modern classic.

Note

1. In Tom McAfee, *Whatever Isn't Glory: Short Stories* (St. Louis, Mo.: K. M. Gentile, 1980); also in *Points of View: An Anthology of Short Stories* (New York: New American Library, 1966).

References

Rosenblatt, Louise. *Literature as Exploration,* 3d rev. ed. New York: Noble & Noble, 1968.
———. *The Reader, the Text, the Poem.* Carbondale: Southern Illinois Univ. Press, 1978.

Confronting Shakespeare's Language in *A Midsummer Night's Dream*

Barbara Hilliard
Thornlea Secondary School, Thornhill, Ontario

Students invariably approach their first Shakespeare text expecting the language to be difficult. To help them, we often use school texts filled with explanatory notes written by knowledgeable editors, and play recordings of performances by skilled artists. Unfortunately, these measures *remove* students from the language and encourage them to be passive and to rely on others to interpret the language for them. Paraphrasing then creeps more and more frequently into class discussion and the original richness of the text is lost.

In my course on Shakespeare's comedies for tenth-grade students, I consider my first job to be convincing these students that Shakespeare's language is not really as hard as they have been told. I often introduce the course with the following exercise from *A Midsummer Night's Dream*. When the students first come in, I give them a brief introduction to the mechanicals and their thespian aspirations before dividing the class into four groups. Each group receives a series of cards, containing the speeches of: 1. Handing Out the Parts (act 1, scene 2), 2. The First Rehearsal (3, 1, ll. 1-69), and 3. and 4. The Performance Before the Duke, Parts 1 and 2 (5, 1, 114-269 and 270-357). The students' task is to assemble the cards, each containing a single speech, in order. (The use of cards is more important than I at first realized. Ingenious students can work at joining cut or tear lines on paper, without examining the words at all.) I check their completed versions, and when Shakespeare's play has been reconstructed the students go on to prepare a dramatic presentation of these scenes.

This process takes several days and culminates in the staging of the scenes. Of course, judged by theater standards, they aren't usually very good. However, the students have had a good time in their first meeting with Shakespeare's language and are confident from the beginning of the course that they can read this language without notes. Then, when these scenes come up again as we read through the text, the lines are already familiar to some extent and reinforce this feeling of confidence. The students have become acquainted with the other members of their groups as well, and have gotten over the initial nervousness of acting in front of the class. After all, everyone has had to do it, and the mechanicals, fortunately, are supposed to seem awkward. A focus has also been established for this work as theater, to be seen and not just read.

This exercise can be adapted for any of the plays, but I have chosen *A Midsummer Night's Dream* for several reasons. The process of the mechanicals' production can be done from beginning to end without needing any important plot or character elements from the rest of the play. Their simple prose and many questions within each well-defined segment provide enough clues to keep the task a manageable one. Even more important to me is the message these mechanicals bring to us about Shakespeare's understanding of the nature of theater and the role of both the audience and the actors.

Pyramus and Thisby, the play within the play, takes up most of the fifth act once the main action of the play is over, indicating that Shakespeare must have intended some significance in this smaller play itself. The mechanicals have no imagination and can't understand the role of illusion in the theater. Their play fails, and so shows us, by example, how *not* to produce a play. By including an unreceptive audience on stage, Shakespeare also makes clear that the responsibility for creating a successful play must be shared by both actors and audience. Students are made aware of this responsibility during the performance of their own scenes, in which they must act as both actors and audience. These scenes also introduce students to the "superior awareness"[1] that Bertrand Evans sees as the basis of Shakespeare's dramatic method in the comedies. Along with Puck, from his position of all-seeing superiority, we look down and laugh at "what fools these mortals [and immortals] be."

Puck may be the ideal English student. "I'll be an auditor/An actor too perhaps, if I see cause" (3, 1, 77-78), he decides as he watches the mechanicals in the woods. Here Shakespeare has taken a bare stage in the harsh light of day and created a magical, moonlit forest, simply through the richness of his language. With this exercise, I hope to set up a relaxed atmosphere in which students can, with Puck, be auditors of that language and at times become actors in their exploration of that world.

Note

1. Bertrand Evans, *Shakespeare's Comedies* (Oxford: The Clarendon Press, 1960).

Court of Appeals: An Approach to Teaching Aeschylus' *Oresteia*

Constance Hines Solari
Sacred Heart Preparatory, Menlo Park, California

The teaching of Aeschylus' *Oresteia* at any grade level provides an interesting challenge, but teaching it at an all-girls high school has required me to place a larger emphasis on Aeschylus' stridently patriarchal point of view. Every year's study of the trilogy brings with it at least one—and usually several—protests from my class that a great obscenity has been perpetrated at the play's end; that Athena and Apollo practice a shameless policy of "male chauvinist" appeasement in their relegation of the Furies to the position of Eumenides; and that Clytemnestra never really gets a fair shake!

Partly to quell the anger, partly to arouse some reaction in that portion of the class that has failed to be moved by such a statement as Athena's "I am always for the male / with all my heart, . . . / so, in a case where the wife has killed her husband, lord / of the house, her death shall not mean much to me," or Apollo's "The mother is no parent of that which is called / her child, but only the nurse of the new-planted seed / that grows. The parent is he who mounts,"[1] I have come up with a project that I feel does both. At the same time, it forces students to look closely at key passages from the three plays, to practice the art of explication, to summarize, to rebut, and to separate their own intellectual baggage from that of Aeschylus. For best results, this project should follow a lengthy discussion of the trilogy and an introductory unit on mythological archetypes and archetypal criticism.

Using a format similar to that of a debate, I split the class in half and ask each half to pretend that it must defend either Clytemnestra or Orestes in a mock trial. Their specific instructions run something like this:

> In two days, you will be a part of a debate team that will argue in favor of either Clytemnestra or Orestes. The debate will entail your pretending that you are a lawyer for one side or the other.
>
> As tonight's homework, select a passage from each play of Aeschylus' trilogy, passages you feel defend your client's course of action in the trilogy.

Your team will meet tomorrow to select which three passages it will adopt for the debate on Friday. At this point, you will work with your team:

1. to organize a five-minute explication of each passage in terms of how it supports your side;
2. to select a spokesperson for each "explication" segment of the debate; and
3. to select a spokesperson who can present a *summary* of your argument, as well as a *rebuttal* to the opposition's arguments. Your spokesperson will have only seven (7) minutes in which to organize input from teammates (who will have taken copious notes during the presentations!), so choose carefully.

The debate will follow the format below:

10:05-10:10 Formal presentation of problem by instructor
10:10-10:13 Presentation 1 (from *Agamemnon*) for Orestes
10:13-10:16 Presentation 1 (from *Agamemnon*) for Clytemnestra
10:16-10:19 Presentation 2 (from *Libation Bearers*) for Orestes
10:19-10:22 Presentation 2 (from *Libation Bearers*) for Clytemnestra
10:22-10:25 Presentation 3 (from *Eumenides*) for Orestes
10:25-10:28 Presentation 3 (from *Eumenides*) for Clytemnestra
10:28-10:35 Organization of summary and rebuttal
10:35-10:40 Summary and rebuttal (for Orestes)
10:40-10:45 Summary and rebuttal (for Clytemnestra)

Note that your job here is to argue in terms of which character is more justified in such a course of action (murder!), using Aeschylus as your point of departure, but not limiting yourself to his point of view. In other words, "intellectual baggage" should include your own thoughts, as well as Aeschylus', and your argument should reflect values in the late twentieth century, as you see them.

As a final exercise, I am asking you to write a summary of the exercise that:

1. resolves the question of guilt from your point of view, based on (a) your understanding of the plays and (b) your reaction to the debate;

2. states to what extent your conclusion is in line with Aeschylus' own conclusion, as it is written in *Eumenides;* and

3. explains why 2 might differ from 1. Here you may want to consider the *mythos* of the twentieth century as it concerns male-female roles and relationships, attitudes toward war, the definition of justice, the nature of parenthood, attitudes toward religion, and so on.

By closely scrutinizing Aeschylus' frame of reference, the students become not only more interested readers, but more critical ones. Rather than approach his work with that reverential awe which all too often kills the classics for high-school students, I prefer to treat it (at least for a few days) as a work with some very questionable underlying assumptions. In asking students to analyze and respond to these assumptions, I encourage them to examine their own assumptions on several contemporary (and very "hot") issues. For this reason alone, I think the project has at least as much—if not more—relevance for a coeducational, or even an all-male, high school.

Note

1. *Aeschylus One: Oresteia, Agamemnon, the Libation Bearers, the Eumenides,* trans. Richmond Lattimore (Chicago: Univ. of Chicago Press, 1953), 161, 158.

All the World's a Cave

David E. Tabler
Ann Arbor Pioneer High School, Ann Arbor, Michigan

In teaching Plato's Simile of the Cave to my advanced high-school seniors as the gateway to a discussion of Platonic philosophy, a major problem was to present this abstract material vividly enough that they might quickly grasp Plato's basic concept. I made the cave vivid for my students by using *them* as my props, leading them to participate in Plato's famous and crucial analogy.

I used this technique when lecturing before a group of eighty or ninety students, but it could be used with any size group. Because our lecture room had tiered rows of seats, it was perfect for the cave illusion, but this was just good luck and is certainly not essential to the success of the approach.

To create the setting, I lowered a large movie screen in the front of the room, and placed in front of it six chairs, facing the screen with their backs to the class. Behind them I put an overhead projector. When I asked for volunteers I quickly got six students to come and sit in the chairs facing the screen. (I might add that this was always done impromptu on the students' part. I needed a spontaneity from them that I could not have gotten with any rehearsal, or even a warning.)

"This room is a cave," I announced, once the six were seated, and I dimmed the lights. "In front of you is the wall of the cave, and seated facing it are six cave-dwellers. They are going to follow my directions, and you are going to think about the situation in which they live and its implications for us all."

I cautioned the six "cave people" that they were chained to their chairs and no matter what happened could not turn around until I freed them. They could see only the wall/screen and what was reflected on it, unaware of anything behind them. I then switched on the projector, explaining that this was a fire, casting its light on the wall of the cave. At my request another student or two stood beside the projector and made shadow animals and figures in the harsh light. The students on the chairs discussed the shadow reflections on the screen, named them, pointed at them. I explained that this was their total reality—that they knew nothing of the projector or the shadow-makers.

"For reasons unknown," I announced, "one of our prisoners is freed of his chains." And I selected one of the six, whispering, "Do exactly what I tell you."

As the student stood up, turned around, faced the projector, blinked in its light, and registered surprise at the "new" knowledge suddenly available, I explained the situation of Plato's freed prisoner, astonished, blinded, and frightened by dimensions of truth he had never before imagined. I led my budding philosopher past the projector and slowly, stumblingly, up the steps of the tiered seats, continuing to explain Plato's analogy as I went. Upon reaching the top of the rows of seats, I asked what might happen if he were able to go through a door there and into the daylight world outside. I then led my prisoner back to the chair in the front of the room.

By so personalizing and making visual the dilemma of the philosopher, I could help students perceive his situation once back in the cave. They understood the dual level of existence Plato presents. They were eager to suggest behaviors for their "enlightened" classmate. ("Just look after the others. You know more than they do." "Keep it to yourself. They wouldn't understand, anyway." "What do you *care* what they think?" "Try to explain to them. Help them." "Better yet, try to get them to go out, too. Use your new knowledge to free them.")

Questions led the class to understand the basic implications of Plato's metaphor. "If Joe is a *teacher,* what might he do? What if the others don't *want* to leave their safe and comfortable chairs? Should he force them? Those stairs are hard to climb. And remember how bright that light was and how it hurt his eyes at first?"

"Suppose Sue is a politician? Does she have a right to govern them just because she knows that the shadows are only shadows? Does she have the responsibility to?"

"And what if Mae is an evangelical religious leader? Or suppose she's the more mystical type? What would she do then?"

"And what do you suppose will become of Tim if Jerry has money invested in those shadows? How will he react if Tim keeps telling everyone how worthless they are? What if Anne makes her living drawing and selling copies of the shadows? Will Tim still enjoy them?"

"Will they let our hero lead them to the Truth? Or will they laugh at him, or be afraid of him, or consider him a harmless crank? Will they allow him to be a benevolent dictator? Or will they try to get rid of him by putting him in jail, or shooting him, or crucifying him, or making him drink hemlock?"

The vividness of actually seeing their classmates in the cave situation, walking through the metaphor, and the intellectual involvement of being asked to predict a conclusion to the little drama they had just witnessed, caused this lesson to stand out in my students' minds. To this day, students I had several years ago recall with pleasure and accuracy their dramatic experience in Plato's cave.

Paraphrasing a Dialogue from *Pride and Prejudice*

Allan J. Ruter
Glenbrook South High School, Glenview, Illinois

Any study of *Pride and Prejudice* must examine the hallmarks of Jane Austen's literary technique—her wit, her irony, her characterizations, her syntactical complexity. Without undue effort on their part, my college preparatory seniors can understand and appreciate these hallmarks. Perhaps because they focus too closely on these aspects of Austen's writing, however, they easily lose sight of the realism inherent in the novel's theme and conflicts. To impress them with the timelessness of the author's fictional situations in *Pride and Prejudice,* I devote two days in class to a dialogue-paraphrasing activity.

Before explaining anything about the activity on the first day, I ask two of my best readers—one boy, one girl—to prepare for the next day's class the dialogue right in the middle of the novel in which Darcy proposes to Elizabeth for the first time and Elizabeth refuses. After these two students leave the classroom to rehearse their lines, I divide the remaining boys and girls into two groups each. I ask one group of boys and one group of girls to examine Darcy's and Elizabeth's lines in this dialogue, respectively, and paraphrase each line into modern standard English. Then I ask the remaining group of boys and group of girls to examine the scene similarly and to convert the dialogue into modern English slang. Each group records its paraphrasing neatly so that one of its members, selected by the group, will be able to present these lines in modern reenactments on the following day in class. The students spend the remainder of this class period working in their groups, while I nose around exercising a bit of editorial discretion here and suggesting a better word there—but only when asked. Also, I invite each boys' group to decide the setting for its "proposal," since the men of Jane Austen's day almost always had the say as to where they would pop the question. After the boys have determined the settings, I notify the corresponding girls' groups.

On the second day, I bring to class a stereo and records that will serve as appropriate soundtracks for the presentations. The students usually need at least ten minutes at the beginning of class to make some final alterations in their paraphrasing. (To preserve the spontaneity of real conversation in the dialogues, I do not allow either of the "modern couples" to rehearse together.) Then, after we arrange our desks in a haphazardly theatrical way, I introduce the first pair of readers, who present Austen's scene as she herself wrote it, accompanied by some tasteful Bach or Brahms. The dialogue ends, the applause dies, and I set the stage for the next presentation—this one in modern standard English, with the lush sounds of *The Way We Were* film soundtrack in the background. Scattered laughter makes this reenactment longer than the previous one. After applause and giggles subside, I introduce the last version of Darcy's proposal to Elizabeth, by far the noisiest and funniest version—modern English slang. (I have found that Stevie Nicks's "Stop Draggin' My Heart Around" is as apt a musical helper for this presentation as one could desire.)

After they have discussed, written, sat through, and presented these three renditions of Jane Austen's brief but important episode, my students are undeniably surprised—some are even chagrined!—to have had so much fun while learning so much about a classic literary work and the differing levels of our language.

5 Units for Specific Titles: College

Teaching the Book of Job
to College Freshmen

Nancy B. Black
Brooklyn College, New York

> There lived in the land of Uz a man of blameless and upright life
> named Job, who feared God and set his face against wrongdoing.
> He had seven sons and three daughters; and he owned seven thou-
> sand sheep and three thousand camels, five hundred yoke of oxen
> and five hundred asses, with a large number of slaves. Thus Job was
> the greatest man in all the East.

Thus begins the Book of Job in a straightforward introduction to what
seems at first a simple tale. The reader can have no doubt about what
kind of a man Job is—"blameless," "upright," "the greatest man in all the
East." The simplicity and directness of tone in the opening seem to suggest
a fairy tale is to follow, but it soon becomes clear that the author has in
mind something more original and complex.

The Book of Job is a challenging reading assignment for most college
freshmen: challenging because of its length; challenging because of its
unusual form—a series of long, rather static speeches; challenging because
of the vastness of the human questions it raises. It was especially challenging for the students to whom I was teaching it—a group of freshmen
who had failed the minimum competency tests in reading and writing
upon entrance to college.

To give my students a preview of what kind of a work they were about
to study, I asked them to stop and take a few moments to skim through
the whole book and tell me what they could perceive, merely by skimming,
about what was to follow. Gradually, with some prodding, they began to
make a few observations: they could see that the story had an opening
and closing section in prose and that the rest of the story was in poetry;
they noticed the italicized headings in the Oxford Study Edition we were
using, and they saw that the headings provided a summary of the whole
book; within individual sections, they saw further subdivisions where the

author wrote: "Then Eliphaz the Temanite began" or "Then Job answered." Finally they could see that the center of the book consisted of a series of long, formal, poetic speeches, eighteen in all, three from each of Job's "friends," Eliphaz, Bildad, and Zophar, with Job's responses to each. Thus the work was a series of dialogues with Job, not exactly drama, not really like anything they had ever read before.

With this overview in place, I turned to my principal topic—the dramatic qualities of the book. I found one student willing to read aloud; after an initial lackluster reading I asked the class if the passage would be read differently if performed publicly. This idea brought a consciousness of audience and immediate changes in tone of voice and demeanor by subsequent readers. Someone suggested the action being described by the narrator might be pantomimed while the narrator spoke, and one student experimented a bit with this as the class looked on in approval.

We continued to read aloud, section by section, stopping periodically to list on the board what we were learning about the principal characters—thus far, God, Satan, and Job. As we identified characteristics for each, the students were asked how that characteristic might be accented in a dramatic performance for an audience. Where would we place God and Satan on the stage? How would we dress them? How human should they seem? Should God sound proud of his servant Job when he says to Satan: "You will find no one like him on earth, a man of blameless and upright life, who fears God and sets his face against wrongdoing"? Should Satan be sarcastic when he responds: "Have you not hedged him round on every side with your protection, him and his family and all his possessions? Whatever he does you have blessed, and his herds have increased beyond measure. But stretch out your hand and touch all that he has, and then he will curse you to your face." Or perhaps neither character should be thought of as a human, dramatic figure, realistically dressed and placed on stage. Perhaps they should merely be shadows projected onto the back of the stage with accompanying sepulchral voices.

By the end of the first class, the students were beginning to think like directors of a play. They were beginning to see the many dramatic possibilities in the story and to read with more awareness. Job and his friends came alive, for by clarifying the tone of their speech we had a way to perceive their feelings and intentions. Stiff printed words turned into sarcastic barbs, pained regret, or philosophic despair.

The next class on Job focused on the central dialogues between Job and his three friends. I warned the class in advance that, although we had talked about the story as drama, they should not expect too much drama. These speeches are static compared to dialogue in plays intended for dramatic production. I encouraged them, as they read at home, to try to keep in mind the overview we had established in class. Read section by section and take marginal notes, I suggested. For each section locate a key word and ask, "What characteristics of the speaker are revealed? What is the tone of the passage?" "Yes, it's fine to write in the book—it shows you're reading with care, thoughtfully," I explained. They needed only to jot down one-word responses in the margins of their texts. Keeping a focal question in mind and keeping their pencils moving while they read would help keep them reading attentively, I theorized. As added reinforcement, I promised to start the next class by going around the room to check the notes they had written in their books.

Class that next week consisted of a straightforward discussion of the characteristics of Eliphaz, Bildad, and Zophar as revealed in the first cycle of speeches. This is not an easy text through which to study characterization, for one has to pull at the text, read carefully, and dig a little to uncover the subtle differences in the responses of each character to Job's condition. But *because* aspects of character are a little harder to discover in this text, reading closely and carefully gained in importance. As we discussed the characters, it was difficult to decide if Eliphaz should be seen as gentle, polite, and comforting, or as rough, forceful, and insensitive to Job's plight. I didn't try to push them toward one view or the other, but encouraged them to tolerate ambiguity and take a "wait and see" attitude. Maybe the text would offer better clues in later speeches of Eliphaz.

The characters of Bildad and Zophar seemed easier to distinguish. Bildad's open anger against Job ("How long will you say such things, / the long-winded ramblings of an old man? / Does God pervert Judgement? / Does the Almighty pervert justice?") made Bildad seem narrow-minded. God is the perfect judge; God is just; so you, Job, must be at fault, he seemed to be saying. With Zophar came a climax to the rebuking of Job in this first cycle of speeches. Zophar is the most forceful of the three men here because he reminds Job of God's great power ("Can you fathom the mystery of God, / can you fathom the perfection of the Almighty?") and of man's inconsequentiality ("You can do nothing . . . you can know nothing").

The real trick to pacing the classes on the Book of Job lay in the fact that, if we were to read the whole book thoroughly, we would have had to repeat the same process of character study that we engaged in for the first cycle of speeches for the second cycle, and again for the third. This could become repetitious and boring. With a more self-reliant group of students, I could have asked them to do this at home, or our discussion of the character of the three friends could have drawn on the larger reading assignment of all three cycles at once. Instead I hit upon a way of changing the pacing and practicing some of the note-taking techniques I had introduced earlier.

In order to discuss the second cycle, I divided the class into groups, one group for each speech, six groups in all. Each group had two questions to answer: What new aspects of character, if any, are revealed in the speech? What are the chief arguments presented? Furthermore, I assigned each person in the group a job: to read the passage aloud, to record the ideas expressed in the small group, or to report back to the whole class. Thus no one could hide behind another person; all had to be active observers of the assigned passage. In this way I broke their traditional expectations of the teacher's role in the classroom. I was removing myself from the ordinary front-and-center position and reformulating the class into small groups. The workshop atmosphere and structure of these activities changed my role from that of director to that of facilitator. It changed their roles from passive listeners to participants in a group activity.

The final week of discussion of the Book of Job focused on God's answer to Job. These classes had a sense of celebration, celebration of their accomplishment in completing the reading of the text and of joy in reciting some of the most beautiful poetry we had read together.

The central question I posed in discussing God's answer from the whirlwind was: "What is the concept of God presented in this section?" In posing this question, I was asking them to make a significant jump in their thinking about the text, from observed detail to abstract concept. In this section God presents a series of questions, beginning with, "Who is this whose ignorant words / cloud my design in darkness?" I wanted to help the students see that these questions emphasized the enormity of God's knowledge in comparison with Job's limited understanding. I wanted to help them see that question after question ("Have you visited the storehouse of the snow / or seen the arsenal where hail is stored. . . . Can you bind the cluster of the Pleiades / or loose Orion's belt?") emphasized the mystery and power of God's realm. And, finally, I wanted to help them see that the culminating image of "the chief of beasts, the crocodile," whom no one but God can subdue, confirmed Job's powerlessness, logically bringing about his repentance.

Earlier I referred to the Book of Job as a challenge. This work was undoubtedly "above grade-level" for the reading abilities of this group of students. Nevertheless, I think it important to present such challenges, for they force students to stretch, to reach a little beyond their limits. This book was an adult story. It treated hard, philosophical questions. By asking them to read this book, I was saying that questions like "What is good?" "What is evil?" "Is God just?" are questions they too, as adults, have to grapple with, and that the study of literature, particularly a book like the Book of Job, can suggest answers to these universal human questions.

From Classic to Modern:
The Marriage Theme in
Pride and Prejudice

Louise Flavin
University of Cincinnati, Ohio

Jane Austen's novels have always been considered classics, and *Pride and Prejudice* is the best-known of them all. This novel, like nearly all of Austen's works, is concerned with the subject of courtship and marriage, and the novel can be seen as a compendium on how to marry well or, in Austen's eighteenth-century language, prudently. The novel is rich in marriage models, both failed and successful—the Bennets and the Gardiners, for instance—and its cast of characters is made up of numerous persons of marriageable age: the five Bennet daughters as well as a best friend, a cousin, a new neighbor and his sister, his friend and his friend's sister, and a whole regiment of redcoats stationed nearby. The scene is set for the unfolding of a story of courtship, intrigue, and even passion. However, college English students, confronted with the at times difficult syntax and unfamiliar language of the novel, often have trouble understanding and enjoying it. As with many classics, students fail to see in it any relevance to their own lives and time. What I propose is looking at the novel from the perspective of young people who face the problem of how to marry (or not to marry if they choose). My approach centers on using Austen's method of character and situational pairings, contrasts and comparisons that set off and define the good marriages and the proper courtships from those that fail. By focusing on students' experiences in their families and among their friends, we arrive at a modern definition of a good marriage relationship that has as its foundation the standards Austen sets forth in *Pride and Prejudice*. The method makes use of student responses, mainly analogies and character vignettes, that bring Austen's characters into the modern era.

By looking at the married partners in the novel, we identify the ingredients of a good marriage and what makes for the model of the failed marriage. Elizabeth, considered a good judge of character and relationships, gives us this analysis of her parents' marriage:

> Had Elizabeth's opinion been all drawn from her own family, she
> could not have formed a very pleasing picture of conjugal felicity or

101

domestic comfort. Her father captivated by youth and beauty, and that appearance of good humour, which youth and beauty generally give, had married a woman whose weak understanding and illiberal mind, had very early in their marriage put an end to all real affection for her. Respect, esteem, and confidence, had vanished for ever; and all his views of domestic happiness were overthrown.[1]

Students will want definitions of some of the abstractions used in Austen's time, for instance that Mrs. Bennet's "weak understanding and illiberal mind" refer to the fact that she is not intelligent, nor has she improved herself over the years by reading and learning. One reason for the lack of "conjugal felicity" in this marriage is that Mrs. Bennet is not as intelligent, well-read, or interested in learning as her husband. When this is discovered by Mr. Bennet, after an initial attraction to her youth, beauty, and good humor, he loses "real affection" for her, a term Austen's readers would interpret to mean true love. Real love is not part of this relationship since Mr. Bennet cannot respect and esteem his wife, an intellectual inferior. Instead of helping his wife to grow intellectually, Mr. Bennet retreats to his library and makes fun of her.

In contrast, we are given the Gardiners, Mrs. Bennet's brother and his wife. Unlike the Bennets, they are equally matched intellectually and, understandably, have a marriage relationship that the Bennet sisters and Austen's readers can respect and admire. Mrs. Gardiner is her husband's equal and remains good-humored, while Mrs. Bennet suffers from a case of nerves and bad spirits. The Gardiners display good judgment and sense in their reaction to Lydia's elopement with Wickham and in their advice to Elizabeth about marriage, while the Bennets evade their responsibility and contribute to Lydia's downfall.

After examining these two models of marriage, the class examines marriage relationships from their own lives, those of parents or friends, even their own. They are asked to speculate, in short papers, on why these couples married each other, why each is successful or has failed, and what would improve the relationship. Though a voluntary exercise on the student's part, this analysis leads to some provocative discussion of the marriages students see around them. Most come to agree with Jane Austen that mutual respect and esteem are highly valued qualities, and they agree that couples need to know each other quite well before marriage if they are to remain in love for a lifetime.

We then discuss the various courtships, potential marriages, and speculative relationships that make up the action of the novel. Mr. Collins and Charlotte's marriage is one students respond to strongly. They easily see Collins as a pompous fool and recognize his motive in approaching any Bennet girl he thinks might have him. He and Charlotte represent the kind of person who will marry anyone, simply to fulfill the need to be married. Many students identify with this pressure to marry; many even fear that, if they don't marry by their early twenties, the chances of finding a partner will be greatly reduced. They talk of the pressure to marry when their friends get engaged or when they are nearing graduation and about to go separate ways. Charlotte's is a sad case, but many can identify with her plight; they feel that her adjustments to Collins and Lady Catherine are ones many married partners have had to make. We are left to speculate how long Charlotte will retain her good humor as her life with a man she cannot respect continues. By contrast, Elizabeth's rejection of Darcy and ten thousand pounds is quite admirable, showing that she is not so desperate as the older Charlotte.

While the courtship of Charlotte and Mr. Collins takes place in a brief time offstage, that of Jane Bennet and Bingley is near the center of the novel's action. This courtship raises the concern that couples know each other well before they become engaged. Darcy's interference in the relationship proves in error, but we can understand his concern for his friend. He had often before seen Bingley in love with pretty girls, and Jane, though she shows much "candour," is too guarded in her emotions, making Darcy suspect she is not really in love with Bingley but wants to marry him for his fortune or because of a superficial attraction. This leads to a discussion on dating and how open couples should be about their feelings. Students also discuss how long a courtship should extend, noting that Jane and Bingley do not marry quickly but only after a test of their love's endurance. They are separated for a year, and yet when they are reunited they find the same attraction to one another as before they parted. What they discover is that, as Elizabeth tells us, "they had for basis the excellent understanding, and super-excellent disposition of Jane, and a general similarity of feeling and taste between her and himself" (3, 13). Mutual respect and esteem again form the basis of a workable relationship.

Elizabeth too is involved in a long courtship, one she does not at first realize she is party to. After nearly a year she learns of her compatability with Darcy:

> She began now to comprehend that he was exactly the man, who, in disposition and talents, would most suit her. His understanding and temper, though unlike her own, would have answered all her wishes. It was an union that must have been to the advantage of both; by her ease and liveliness, his mind might have been softened, his manners improved, and from his judgment, information, and knowledge of the world, she must have received benefit of greater importance. (3, 8)

What emerges from looking at the courtships of Jane and Elizabeth is a definition of the best marriage relationship, one in which partners look up to and respect their mates for mutually compatible qualities, and one in which the love is allowed to mature over a space of time before marriage.

Austen also provides a model of an inappropriate courtship to contrast with those to be admired. Lydia and Wickham represent the couple who, as Elizabeth says, "were only brought together because their passions were stronger than their virtue" (3, 8). Lydia is a younger version of her mother: attractive and good humored, but without either good sense or self-control. Her elopement stimulates much discussion about marriages based on physical attraction or marriages that result from pregnancy. In Austen's time the only honorable thing for Lydia to do, having spent two weeks living with Wickham, would have been to marry. Students readily discuss the alternatives to marriage for someone in Lydia's situation, and many identify with the pressures to marry because of physical attraction.

Finally, young readers are interested in the role of parental advice or interference in a young person's choice of a marriage partner. Many of the characters in *Pride and Prejudice* are in some way involved in giving, taking, or rejecting advice. Darcy interferes on behalf of his friend Bingley and, it turns out, wrongly so. Yet Darcy had also interfered in time to prevent his sister's destruction by Wickham and is responsible for seeing that Wickham marries Lydia. Lady Catherine tells Collins, "You must marry," and sets him in the direction of the five amiable Bennet daughters. Lady Catherine also attempts to prevent Elizabeth from marrying Darcy since she and her sister had designed a marriage between their children, Darcy and Anne. The narrator says of Mrs. Bennet that the "business of her life was to get her daughters married" (1, 1), and she not only promotes the marriage of Jane and Bingley, but also insists Elizabeth marry Mr. Collins. All of these people give advice and, luckily, much of it is ignored. Austen does not want readers to see all advice and interference as bad, however, and she includes some sound advice on marrying from one of her most admired characters, Mrs. Gardiner:

> "You are too sensible a girl, Lizzy, to fall in love merely because you are warned against it; and, therefore, I am not afraid of speaking openly. Seriously, I would have you be on your guard. Do not involve yourself, or endeavour to involve him in an affection which the want of fortune would make so very imprudent. I have nothing to say against *him;* he is a most interesting young man; and if he had the fortune he ought to have, I should think you could not do better. But as it is—you must not let your fancy run away with you. You have sense, and we all expect you to use it." (2, 3)

While the novel goes on to prove that Elizabeth can, in fact, do *much* better, the advice is nonetheless sound, and provocative to young people. How many students can admit to having continued dating or even having married someone solely because it was "warned against"? This passage also treats an issue many students find repellent in Austen's fiction, the concern for marrying someone with a fortune. Students must be made to understand the difficulty of living as a gentleman or lady during this time if the couple did not have income or inheritance. A match was considered imprudent if a couple married for love without any regard for how they would live. Certainly, Austen equally condemns the fortune-hunter who marries solely for money; but Mrs. Gardiner's advice, students readily agree, is still sound. They can recount their own concerns with completing college or getting established in their jobs or careers before marrying and beginning families. A marriage based on love alone often becomes a disaster when the problems of money become a reality. The prudent marriage in Jane Austen's time carries the same definition in modern times.

While this novel can, and should be, discussed for other themes and issues, notably that of the title, I find the novel's most relevant theme to be courtship and marriage. Jane Austen's perceptive look at whom and why we marry is just as insightful today as it was when the novel was written. For students the novel becomes a classic for modern times.

Note

1. Jane Austen, *Pride and Prejudice,* ed. R. W. Chapman (London: Oxford Univ. Press, 1965), vol. 2, ch. 19. All further references to this text are indicated by volume and chapter numbers within parentheses.

The Bible as Social Text: Examining the Roles of Women

Duane H. Roen
University of Arizona, Tucson

There are, of course, many ways to consider the Bible as a collection of literature. One could teach it through units on genre since it includes a diversity of literary genres. One could teach themes that recur throughout the Old Testament or the New Testament. One could also, however, treat the Bible by subject area.

In my own experience in teaching the Bible as literature, I have discovered that students are intrigued by the subject of women's roles as portrayed in the Bible. By considering these roles carefully, we can help college students to understand the cultural contexts in which the Bible was written. By directing students to appropriate written histories, and perhaps even by drawing on the expertise of the history department, we can help students to understand those contexts even better. Then it becomes possible to compare and contrast those contexts with contemporary ones—contexts that assign roles to women in literature and in real life.

A helpful resource for planning a unit on the roles of women in the Bible is Frank S. Mead's *Who's Who in the Bible* (Old Tappan, N. J.: Fleming H. Revell, 1973). Mead, a widely published religious scholar, has identified 250 major figures from the Bible; only forty-two of them are women. Of those forty-two women, all but a few are identified by their relationships to men (e.g., wife of, mother of, sister of, daughter of). Mead's procedures for identifying these women should raise several questions: Did Mead, a man in a sexist culture, reflect his own culture's values when he identified these biblical characters by their relationships to men? Or, did Mead's identification procedures simply provide us with greater insights into the cultures portrayed in the Bible? These two questions might serve to guide students through the entire unit.

The forty-two women Mead identifies are listed here. Some appear more than once.

Genesis: Eve, Hagar, Sarah, Rebekah, Rachel, Leah, Zilpah

Exodus: Shiphrah, Jochebed, Thermouthis, Miriam

Joshua: Rahab

Judges: Deborah, Delilah

Ruth: Naomi, Ruth

I Samuel: Hannah, Witch of Endor, Merab, Michal, Abigail

II Samuel: Merab, Michal, Abigail, Bathsheba, Rizpah

I Chronicles: Bathsheba

I Kings: Bathsheba, Queen of Sheba, Jezebel

II Kings: Jezebel, Athaliah

Esther: Vashti, Zeresh, Esther

Matthew: Mary of Nazareth, Mary Magdalene, Claudia Procula

Mark: Mary of Nazareth, Mary Magdalene

Luke: Mary of Nazareth, Mary Magdalene, Elizabeth, Anna, Joanna, Martha, Mary of Bethany

John: Mary of Nazareth, Mary Magdalene, Martha, Mary of Bethany

Acts: Lydia, Priscilla, Diana

Romans: Priscilla, Phoebe

I Corinthians: Priscilla, Chloe

II Corinthians: Priscilla

I Timothy: Priscilla

II Timothy: Priscilla

In approaching the subject of the roles of women in the Bible, teachers might ask students to consider several questions, in addition to those raised earlier. Some of those questions include the following:

1. Has Mead overlooked any female biblical characters?

2. What are the similarities and differences in the roles of biblical women and contemporary female literary characters? How can those similarities and differences be explained?

3. How do particular female characters fit into the Bible as a whole collection of literature?

There are a number of books that help to establish a sense of the cultures in which the books of the Bible were written. These books also, of course, help to provide some insights into roles of women in biblical cultures. One of the most helpful of such books is *The Bible Almanac* (New York: Thomas Nelson, 1980), edited by James J. Packer, Merrill C. Tenney, and William White, Jr. In addition to providing many cultural insights, the book includes sketches of all the characters in the Bible. Equally helpful are Merrill T. Gilbertson's *The Way It Was in Biblical Times* (Minneapolis: Augsburg Publishing House, 1959) and W. W. Heaton's *Everyday Life in Old Testament Times* (London: B. T. Batsford, 1956).

To gauge the cultural bias of Mead's treatment of biblical characters, teachers and students may wish to consult and discuss entries in one or more of the following reference books, each of which is more comprehensive than Mead's *Who's Who in the Bible*. Albert E. Sims and George Dent have compiled an easy-to-use *Who's Who in the Bible: An A B C Cross Reference of Names of People in the Bible* (New York: The Philosophical Library, 1960). Also useful are George M. Alexander's *The Handbook of Biblical Personalities* (Greenwich, Conn.: The Seabury Press, 1962) and William P. Barker's *Everyone in the Bible* (Westwood, N. J.: Fleming H. Revell, 1966).

Of course, there are also sources that offer broader views of attitudes toward women. One interesting title is Vern L. Bullough's *The Subordinate Sex: A History of Attitudes Toward Women* (Urbana: Univ. of Illinois Press, 1973). A more focused book is *Religion and Sexism: Images of Women in the Jewish and Christian Traditions* (New York: Simon & Schuster, 1974), edited by Rosemary Radford Ruether. A book that allows for a direct comparison of female biblical characters and women in real life is Norma Olin Ireland's *Index to Women of the World from Ancient to Modern Times: Biographies and Portraits* (Westwood, Mass.: F. W. Faxon, 1970).

Some English teachers might find themselves in schools or courses in which it is impossible to teach the type of unit described here. However, for those who find it possible to teach the Bible as a social text, rather than a religious one, it seems reasonable to consider a currently important social issue, like the evolution of the roles of women.

Unraveling "Childe Roland"

Earl B. Brown, Jr.
Radford University, Radford, Virginia

For many students the only way to approach a poem is through the meaning of the words. If the meaning eludes them either because of complicated syntax or compressed imagery, they do not know how to proceed. Even our best college students occasionally find themselves in this predicament. What they often do is what they have been taught—find a particular poetic device to pull them through. They will look at structure or structural devices, at rhyme scheme or meter, at figurative devices or imagery. When these fail, they too are ready to quit. One way to help our students over the threshold into understanding is a device I call "pulling a thread." Pulling a thread can certainly involve using a particular poetic device, but more often it involves using a detail, for instance the poem's title or one of its key words, as a means to understanding.

The way this device works is fairly simple. We take the most obvious detail in the poem—whether it be the title or an arresting detail (the mirror in "The Lady of Shalott" for instance)—and brainstorm it. After the class creates a list of possible associations this idea has, we return to the poem to look at how our idea will fit into its context. We can usually eliminate several of these associations, leaving us with only a few to test more fully in the poem. Such a device leads to meaning in Browning's poem, "Childe Roland to the Dark Tower Came," which students often find difficult to comprehend.

At the beginning of class discussion on this poem, I ask my students what they think the poem's title means. The students invariably ask what a "childe" is. After I tell them, they then talk about a knight-to-be coming to a tower. Some of the students notice that the tense is past, that, in fact, he has already come to the tower. Others ask why he has come to the tower, and still others, why a tower at all. The students, having exhausted the possibilities, are now asked which thread they would like to pull first. They usually say the tower.

We brainstorm "tower." I typically get the following responses: a tower is a fortress—it protects people; a tower is a jail—it imprisons people; soon thereafter, knights rescue fair damsels imprisoned in towers; a tower is tall—it affords a vantage point from which to look out over the landscape; a tower can isolate people from each other—as in an "ivory tower"; a tower is a place for self-exile; and a tower is gray and round. At this point we generally stop. We look at our list and see from the given context which associations fit. In stanza 31, lines 181-84, we learn about this tower: "The round squat turret, blind as the fool's heart, / Built of brown stone, without a counterpart / In the whole world." From this information we try to eliminate several of our associations. What strikes the students first is that this tower is not tall; thus, it will afford no vantage point. Given its lack of height, it also would not be effective as a fortress or prison—it is too easy to scale. And it certainly is neither gray nor ivory.

In frustration we decide to pull a different thread. If knowing what a tower is will not help us into the poem, perhaps knowing why Childe Roland wanted to come here will. We again search through the poem. In stanzas 4 and 7 Childe Roland reflects on his search for the dark tower:

> For, what with my whole world-wide wandering,
>   What with my search drawn out through years, my hope
>   Dwindled into a ghost not fit to cope
> With that obstreperous joy success would bring,
> I hardly tried now to rebuke the spring
>   My heart made, finding failure in its scope.
>   (ll. 19-24)

> Thus, I had so long suffered in this quest,
>   Heard failure prophesied so oft, been writ
>   So many times among "The Band"—to wit,
> The knights who to the Dark Tower's search
>   addressed
> Their steps—that just to fail as they, seemed
>   best,
>   And all the doubt was now—should I be fit?
>   (ll. 37-42)

We can find no reason for Childe Roland's search other than the desire in all knights to complete their quest. Although we feel that Childe Roland isn't telling us the whole truth here, we do not know how to find it out.

Again, we turn to the poem. We have discussed in previous class periods on Robert Browning what a dramatic monologue is, that our only way into the poetic material is through the eyes of the speaker, Childe Roland, and that there is an implied audience as well as some development through the poem which leads to the speaker's greater understanding of himself vis-à-vis his world. Perhaps that is why we feel that there are reasons for his quest that he's not telling us, though we can only judge from what he does tell us. In other dramatic monologues—such as "Andrea del Sarto," "My Last Duchess," and "The Bishop Orders His Tomb at Saint Praxed's Church"—we remember that on close observation of the details of the poem we had discovered a disparity between the way the speaker saw the world and the way the world actually is. Could such a disparity exist here? Is the world as bleak and diseased as Childe Roland says? Are "hoary cripples" out to deceive him (st. 1); is the grass like "hair / In leprosy" (st. 13); is the horse really "wicked," deserving of "such pain" (st. 13-14); and did he really step on "a dead man's cheek" and spear a baby (st. 21)?

We now return to our previous associations for the tower. Perhaps, we speculate, Childe Roland fears he is unable to see his world as it really is. He hopes that by climbing to the top of the dark tower he will be able to gain the necessary distance that will allow him to understand the nature of his world. This would explain his reason for seeking the tower as well as his frustration at finding it squat, affording no perspective on his world. His personification at this point is revealing: the tower is truly "blind as the fool's heart." The tower is not only blind but dark. It offers no clarity; from its height, Childe Roland is not able to gain a clear vision of his world. Unable to see his world clearly, Childe Roland now has few options; he can either admit that he will never understand and give up or he can die in his quest. Despite the fact that he can see his death before him in the leering men gathered around the hillside to see the last of him (ll. 199-200), he does not surrender: "and yet / Dauntless the slug-horn to my lips I set / and blew. '*Childe Roland to the Dark Tower came*' " (ll. 202-4). The seemingly enigmatic ending to the poem becomes clear; unable to see his world whole, Childe Roland will blow his challenge to that world. Like earlier Victorian heroes, he is going "to strive, to seek, to find, and not to yield" (Tennyson, "Ulysses," l. 70).

Our thread has led us to this point, but is this interpretation of "Childe Roland" valid? Does it echo other Browning themes or themes of other Victorian writers in general? We have discovered that this poem reveals the uncertainties of the Victorian world and Browning's belief that people must press forward, despite those uncertainties, even if they don't know where they are going. Such a view of life is presented in many other Browning poems, from Andrea del Sarto's "A man's reach should exceed his grasp, / Or what's a heaven for" (ll. 96-97) (though intended ironically by Browning); to the statement of the horseman in "The Last Ride Together" who will "ride, ride together, forever ride" (l. 110) despite the forces ranged against him and his lover; to the Bishop ordering his tomb, realizing full well the more he cajoles his "nephews" the less they will heed his dying requests (ll. 114ff.).

But Browning is not the only poet who speaks of pressing forward despite the uncertainties. Alfred, Lord Tennyson in "Ulysses" has his hero utter the most famous lines of perseverance in the language (l. 70) and his voice in *In Memoriam A.H.H.* expresses this same need to survive despite the death of his friend Hallam. Matthew Arnold, too, comments on the Victorian world: he sees humanity "wandering between two worlds, one dead, / The other powerless to be born" ("Stanzas from the Grande Chartreuse," ll. 85-86); or he sees people as "children bathing on the shore, / Buried a wave beneath, / The second wave succeeds, before / We have had time to breathe" ("Stanzas in Memory of the Author of Obermann," ll. 73-76). Arnold's solution, like those of Browning and Tennyson, is to persevere: the speaker of "Dover Beach" tells his beloved:

> Ah, love, let us be true
> To one another! for the world, which seems
> To lie before us like a land of dreams,
> So various, so beautiful, so new,
> Hath really neither joy, nor love, nor light,
> Nor certitude, nor peace, nor help for pain;
> (ll. 29-34)

and the speaker of "Rugby Chapel" urges his followers "On, to the bound of the waste, / On to the city of God" (ll. 207-8). But it's not only the Victorian poets who realize the need for insight. George Eliot in *Middlemarch* speaks to the same point early in her novel when she has Dorothea comment, "Those provinces of masculine knowledge seemed to her a standing ground from which all truth could be seen more truly."[1]

What we have seen is that if we pull a thread, a poem that many students consider to be opaque can be unraveled, unraveled in a way not only to clarify itself but many other poems as well. Even without the Victorian context, our understanding of "Childe Roland to the Dark Tower Came" has been increased. Not all problems have been solved, but we have made a beginning. This kind of beginning is available for most literary works, for all we must do is pull a thread and see where it leads.

Note

1. George Eliot, *Middlemarch* (New York: New American Library, n.d.), 64.

Hawthorne's *Scarlet Letter:*
A Paradigm for Discussion

Lynne P. Shackelford
Furman University, Greenville, South Carolina

"Write a five-hundred-word essay on the meaning of the *A* in Nathaniel Hawthorne's *Scarlet Letter.*" Thus began my own eleventh-grade entrée into the world of literary symbolism, as I and my classmates, soulmates of Hester Prynne, felt branded ourselves with the dreadful A—in this case, signifying Assignment. Brooding on the gloomy abstractions of sin and guilt, we analyzed the badge on Hester's breast, discussed Pearl as a living embodiment of the scarlet letter, debated the minister's night vision of his guilt projected upon the heavens, and concluded our papers with a succinct paragraph on Hester's tombstone. The only problem was that in the task of symbol-searching we forgot that Hawthorne's romance is first and foremost a study of human relationships and the complex emotions of despair, anger, grief, regret, love, pride, fear, and loneliness with which we all must grapple.

Now that I am teaching *The Scarlet Letter* myself, I try to help college students see the work's relevance to their own lives by reminding them that Hawthorne presents us with a romantic triangle: a woman married to one man has an affair with another and as a result has an illegitimate child. In fact, I actually diagram the novel as a triangle with Hester at its apex, her husband Roger Chillingworth at one of the angles, her lover Arthur Dimmesdale at the other, and her daughter Pearl in the center as the means by which the sin of adultery is exposed. The class then focuses on three series of discussion questions based upon this triangular structure. Students may discuss all of the questions together or be divided into three groups, each concentrating on one set of questions.

Section 1: Motivations

The first set of questions examines how and why the three adult characters are brought together. Seemingly separated in their first appearance in the novel, with Hester on the scaffold, Chillingworth on the outskirts of the crowd, and Dimmesdale on the balcony, among the magisterial and ministerial elite, the three are, however, inextricably linked.

Hester and Chillingworth

1. Why did Hester marry Chillingworth? Did she love him?
2. Why did Chillingworth marry Hester? Were his reasons selfish? Did he love her?
3. Did either Hester or Chillingworth have reason to believe the marriage might be unsuccessful?

Hester and Dimmesdale

1. Why do you think Hester was attracted to Dimmesdale?
2. Why was Dimmesdale attracted to her?
3. Did they love each other?
4. Did Hester have justification for engaging in an affair? Did Dimmesdale?

Chillingworth and Dimmesdale

1. Why does Chillingworth focus his attention on Dimmesdale? Does Chillingworth have any reason to be suspicious of the minister?
2. Why does Dimmesdale spend so much time with Chillingworth? Do the two men have any interests or characteristics in common?

Section 2: Secrecy and Exposure

The next set of questions focuses upon the dichotomy between secrecy and exposure. Ironically, Hester, whose sin is exposed before the stern eyes of the Puritan community as she stands on the scaffold in chapter 2, is the guardian of two important secrets: that Chillingworth is her husband and that Dimmesdale is the father of her child. Secrecy, Hawthorne suggests, does not alleviate suffering; it only further entangles one in a web of duplicities.

Hester and Chillingworth

1. Why does Chillingworth want to keep his identity secret?
2. Why does Hester promise not to acknowledge him as her husband?
3. Does Hester ever regret her decision? If so, why?

Hester and Dimmesdale

1. In chapter 2, Dimmesdale exhorts Hester to confess the name of her lover. Do you think he really wants her to expose his guilt?

2. Why does Hester not confess the name of her fellow sinner?

3. Is Dimmesdale a coward or does he have a good reason for not exposing his guilt? (Look especially at chapter 10.)

4. How does the keeping of the secret affect Dimmesdale? Hester?

5. Why does Dimmesdale finally confess?

Chillingworth and Dimmesdale

1. Of what significance is Chillingworth's role as Dimmesdale's physician? Why is Chillingworth called "the leech"?

2. How does Dimmesdale react to Chillingworth's constant surveillance?

3. How do Chillingworth's and Dimmesdale's views differ concerning the need for earthly confession? (See chapter 10.)

Section 3: Sin and Morality

The third set of questions concentrates upon the characters' moral codes and the consequences of Hester and Dimmesdale's adultery. Agreeing with the Puritans that all people are sinful, Hawthorne reveals the moral weaknesses of his main characters; nevertheless, he refuses to establish absolute standards of good and evil by which we should judge them.

Hester

1. What sin has Hester committed? Why does she sin?

2. Does she take responsibility for her actions? Is she a good mother? Does she care about how her actions have affected Chillingworth and Dimmesdale?

3. Is the punishment the Puritan community imposes upon her justified?

4. How does the punishment change her?

5. Does Hester benefit from her punishment?

Chillingworth

1. Is Roger Chillingworth in any way a sympathetic character?

2. Does he change as the novel progresses?

3. Does Chillingworth sin? How?

Dimmesdale

1. Is Arthur Dimmesdale's only sin adultery?

2. Does Dimmesdale accept responsibility for his actions as well as Hester does for hers?

3. Does Dimmesdale offer Hester sympathy and support?

4. Does Dimmesdale receive salvation?

Evaluation

Discussing these questions promotes a vital engagement of students with Hawthorne's characters. They no longer see Hester, Chillingworth, and Dimmesdale as lifeless fictional entities, but as interesting flesh-and-blood human beings with realistic, complicated problems and emotions. In addition, the discussion encourages students to evaluate their own feelings and values. The first series of questions makes them consider the practical and emotional reasons that we link our lives with others. It examines the consequences of loveless marriage and passionate love outside of marriage. The second set of questions explores the repercussions of presenting a false facade to the world. It asks if guilt is inescapable. The third series focuses upon taking responsibility for one's actions and exposes the dangers of harshly judging others. The ultimate goal of this exercise is for students to recognize that *The Scarlet Letter* transcends its 1640s setting to raise timeless issues about the human condition.

Using the *Odyssey* in Freshman English

Carol Hovanec
Ramapo College of New Jersey, Mahwah, New Jersey

For several years I have included the *Odyssey* by Homer as an assignment in a second-semester freshman English class at Ramapo College, a course designed around the theme of the heroic ideal. Presented here is a method for using the epic, for both expressive and transactional writing.

In a seventeen-week semester, I spend about four weeks on the *Odyssey*. This instruction begins with a class devoted to background, very general "nutshell" comments on Greek history, culture, politics, and religion, the author, and epic characteristics. In a later class I also show slides of places mentioned in or relevant to the poem, such as Mycenae, Cape Sunion, Crete, and Nestor's palace at Pylos, to better fix the reading in the students' consciousness, as well as to highlight the wonders of classical achievement. My ultimate goal, of course, is to use the reading for inspiration in writing, and so my first assignment encourages the students to express themselves orally. Students are directed to read the first eight books and to prepare a series of responses. I ask them to look for several things—something relevant to the 1980s, something also true to their own experience, something upsetting or surprising, something about which they have questions, and a line or passage they consider to be particularly beautiful—and to decide which of the eight books they like best, and why. This exercise provides ample material for one, or even two, sessions as students point out that the emotions, the athletic games, the attitudes toward women, the treatment of the young, and many other aspects have changed little in three thousand years. Also, their questions and our discussion about the mythological references and the lifestyle prove a much more effective underscoring and explanation of my previous background remarks than another lecture. Such a class, with students sitting in a circle, helps them to relax, get to know each other better, gain confidence in speaking in an informal setting, and become less self-conscious about what they do and do not understand about such a reading experience. The writing assignment that evolves from this exercise is expressive. I ask them to develop topics based on the discussion: construct a sketch of someone you know or have known who was suggested by a character in the *Odyssey;* discuss one of society's or your idols in light of our contemporary idea of the hero; write on something that you feel is particularly relevant; point out some of the beautiful passages; or produce a poem or a painting inspired by your reading. In the last instance students must accompany their "masterpieces" with short critiques telling what they hoped to accomplish. I use the papers the day they are turned in for an informal evaluation. Students use numbers in place of names to preserve anonymity; the compositions are then exchanged, and students are to consider whether they like or dislike what they read, and whether their impressions are based on the subject or the presentation. The questions are designed to introduce them to the critical stance, going beyond instantaneous judgment to more reasoned criticism, as well as to let them see and hear what others have written, to give me an opportunity to highlight obvious mistakes, and to further expose them to the happenings of 900 B.C. Most important, the assignment gets them writing and finding connections. As one student commented:

> Today, we do not encounter similar situations, but deal with the same processes of decision-making and determining our future. We all experience fate, whether it be in our careers or personal lives. We often see national decisions made involving "might" and "right" concerning military matters regarding relations of the United States with other nations. We all must learn to be clever in order to "get ahead" in certain situations in our lives. Everyone searches at sometime or another for solutions to their life's adverse conditions. Perhaps Homer's "universal human condition" in the *Odyssey* transcends time only in that we give other explanations, motives, and methods for understanding our fate—at the same time realizing our goals and pursuing our destiny.

The second assignment, following several periods of specific reading and explanation of the remainder of the text, is more traditional, on such topics as the depiction of women, the heroic ideal, verisimilitude, nature, or a comparison to something studied in another course (an anthropologist might be interested in the tribal structure depicted, a theater major the dramatic scenes, and so forth). Since this paper stresses documentation and organization, I instruct students to include short and long quotations, to use footnotes and bibliography, and to pattern their introductory, middle, and concluding paragraphs according to logical standards. In this instance, I lecture on the entire process involved in producing a critical paper, providing samples of professional writing or student examples from previous semesters, and include some exercises on footnoting. When the assignments were turned in the first time this course was taught, I was pleasantly surprised at their quality, coming so early in the semester. For example, a part-time student who wasn't sure he had the ability to undertake college work said in his introduction:

> Imagine a world in which nuclear arms would not proliferate because the people abhorred such devices solely on the grounds that they could obliterate the natural world. A far-fetched idea, yet that might have been a realistic vision of modern society's attitudes toward nature had the classical Greek concept of nature survived. In the *Odyssey,* the author epitomized his ideals of how nature should be and, maybe more importantly, how mankind should relate to nature.

And a business major began this way:

> Homer, the master epic poet, knew that the images of one's mind were the key to capturing and holding his audience's attention. And he knew how to paint these images. He made his audience excited with the spectacular, comfortable with the familiar, and he moved them by the humanness of his characters. The true measure of his genius is marked by the fact that Homer is still as captivating to his audience today as he was three thousand years ago.

Another student, a returning woman, wrote this conclusion to a paper on imagery:

> Everyone has some opinion or explanation of what is real, some perhaps better than others, but, nevertheless, the experience is generic. As a result, if you want to interest a large audience, you use an element everyone can relate to. Such an element was precisely what Homer used while writing the *Odyssey.* Reality is intertwined in the characters, the scenes, the relationships, and the adventures, sometimes subtle, sometimes obvious, but it is unmistakably there.

I had never had students produce such prose so early in the term, if ever, in a composition class; yet the writing was often inspired, and I am convinced that the epic did inspire them, giving them what freshmen never have in the traditional course—ample material to use for support and diction that influences their own expression. No longer were they expected to produce E. B. White essays from the meager experience of their eighteen or so years. Instead of discussing football games, they have Odysseus' exploits to consider; instead of describing disco parties, they can see how Menelaos entertained; instead of characterizing their roommates, they have the delightful Calypso and Nausicaa as models; and instead of arguing yet again about drugs, they can grapple with the question of fate and humanity's destiny.

This unit is followed by others using *Sir Gawain and the Green Knight, Henry V,* and Dickens's *Hard Times,* each work showing the changing view of the hero; each unit also uses the primary, and, in the case of Dickens, some secondary sources to illustrate different stylistic principles such as diction and sentence variety, or for reading practice in summarizing and skimming. This syllabus is a demanding one, but it has been both productive and enjoyable for the students and me. As one student commented on an end-of-semester evaluation, "When I signed up for this course, I thought it would be dull and boring. It has been an eye-opening experience and one which I thoroughly enjoyed. It was challenging and met my expectation of what college should be." Clearly, the classics may be a solution to the dilemma of freshman English.